The Jewish Guide to
Natural
Nutrition

YAAKOV LEVINSON

The Jewish Guide to Natural Nutrition

🕯 FELDHEIM PUBLISHERS Jerusalem / New York

First published 1995
ISBN 0-87306-706-1

Copyright © 1995 by
Yaakov Levinson

All rights reserved.
No part of this publication may be translated, reproduced, stored in a retrieval system or transmitted, in any form or by any means, electronic, mechanical, photocopying, recording, or otherwise, without permission in writing from the publishers.

FELDHEIM PUBLISHERS
POB 35002 / Jerusalem, Israel

200 Airport Executive Park
Nanuet, NY 10954

Printed in Israel

10 9 8 7 6 5 4 3 2 1

To our children

Rabbi CHAIM P. SCHEINBERG
Rosh Hayeshiva "TORAH-ORE"
and Morah Hora'ah of Kiryat Mattersdorf

הרב חיים פינחס שיינברג
ראש ישיבת "תורה-אור"
ומורה הוראה דקרית מטרסדורף

Teves 5755

This book, which outlines the main principles of proper nutrition for the Torah-observant Jew, is long overdue. The author discusses all aspects of eating from the Jewish perspective in an in-depth manner.

It is a well-known teaching that one's learning should lead to proper action (*Bava Kamma* 17a, *Kiddushin* 40b, *Megillah* 27a). I pray that this book will help each reader to deepen his personal service to Hashem in this important area.

I am certain that this book will be of great benefit to Klal Yisrael. Yaakov Levinson is to be commended for his efforts, and I bless him that Hashem should help him succeed in all his endeavors.

With my best wishes,

Chaim Pinchas Scheinberg

רחוב פנים מאירות 2, ירושלים, ת. ד. 6979, טל. (02)-371513, ישראל
2, Panim Meirot St., Jerusalem, P.O.B. 6979, Tel (02)-371513, Israel

Rabbi I. Scheiner
Dean
Kamenitzer Yeshiva of Jerusalem
Zephania St. 51, Jerusalem
Tel. 86512

הרב יצחק שיינר
ראש ישיבת קאמניץ
רחוב צפניי 51, ירושלים
טלפון 86512

Jerusalem
Adar, 5755

Mr. Yaakov Levinson
Rechov Shmuel Hanavi
Jerusalem

Dear friend,

    I read with much interest the proofs of your forthcoming book, concerning diet and health from a true Jewish outlook. Your approach reveals the views of a real expert in the field, also imbued with deep feeling and reverence for Jewish values.

    I remember fondly the time we spent together, while you were so devotedly helping my grandson overcome his problems. I am confident that your book will be warmly received by every Torah-true person, who is also interested in the problems of diet and health, from a Torah imbued perspective.

I. Scheiner

hadassah medical organization

Kiryat hadassah
p.o.b. 12000
il-91120 jerusalem israel
telephone (02) 427427
cables hadassah
telex 26278 hadas il
fax. (02) 434434

הסתדרות מדיצינית הדסה

קרית הדסה
תא דאר 12000
ירושלים 91120
טלפון 427427 (02)
מברקים הדסה
טלקס 26280 הדסה
פקסימיליה 434434 (02)

    Yaakov Levinson has written a very different book on nutrition and dietetics. The distinct "flavor" that distinguishes it from the many other texts that crowd the bookshelves is the unique mixture that he has prepared. It melds an expert's view of nutrition and disease with its special implication and application to religious Jewish tradition.

    This makes it an especially valuable text for patients and families who wish to utilize and apply nutritional knowledge to their own specific needs and within the context of their own religious mores. No less valuable is its place in the armamentarium of the health practitioner whose clientele includes religious Jews with their specific mix of nutritional needs and religious beliefs. This book will be invaluable in providing an appropriate service for them.

Prof. Leon Epstein
Chairman, Dept. of Social Medicine

Contents

Acknowledgments *1*
Preface *3*
Introduction: Jewish roots for natural nutrition *5*

THE NUTRIENTS 9

- *11* The nutrients and their importance
- *15* Weight = energy (a few words on desirable weight)
- *27* The carbohydrates: source of energy
- *39* Fats: storehouse of energy
- *53* Protein: structure of the body
- *59* Vitamins
- *69* Minerals
- *79* Fluid

EATING WELL: Applied principles 83

- *85* General guidelines
- *91* Natural cooking
- *121* Seasoning with herbs and spices

THE SPIRITUAL EFFECTS OF EATING 127

- *128* Spirituality of eating
- *141* Tu b'Shevat: festival of the trees
- *148* The apple: symbol of health

APPENDICES 157

- *158* About calories
- *170* Avoiding a heart attack
- *175* What is a nutritionist?
- *177* Sources

Tables

Vitamins and Minerals　*13*
Desirable Weights for Adults　*18*
Activity and Energy Expenditure　*24*
Dietary Fiber in Foods　*30*
Hidden Sugar in Foods　*35*
Kinds of Fats　*40*
Cholesterol in Foods　*44*
Fat in Foods　*45*
Protein in Foods　*55*
Vitamin C in Foods　*61*
Nutritional Values of Some Fruits　*64*
Calcium in Foods　*70*
Iron in Foods　*73*
Caffeine in Foods　*81*
Apple — nutritional content　*152*
Calorie Tables　*159*
Desirable Weights for Men　*168*
Desirable Weights for Women　*169*

Acknowledgments

My interest in nutrition was first sparked in my early teens by my father's dear friend, Dr. Stanley Levine, who deserves special thanks. The many teachers, professional colleagues, rabbis, students, patients, and friends who molded my career over the years would fill many pages. I thank you all. Outstanding nutrition authorities who have guided me personally include Dr. Janice Neville, D.Sc., R.D., chairperson, Department of Nutrition, Case Western Reserve University, and past president of the American Dietetic Association; Dr. Edith Lerner, Ph.D., R.D., and Dr. Grace Petot, Ph.D., R.D., Department of Nutrition, Case Western Reserve University; Dr. George Blackburn, M.D., Deaconess Hospital (Harvard University); and Kathy King Helm, R.D., Lake Dallas, Texas.

Deepest thanks go to my parents, Dr. and Mrs. Max Levinson, who, besides everything else, supported a professional student for so many years, and to my dear, late grandfather, Irving Jaffe, who was always there with loving encouragement. Special thanks to my wife, Sarah Miriam, who poured vast emotional and intellectual energy into this book and into my entire nutrition career.

I am grateful to Hanoch Teller, dear friend and advisor, and to Marsi Tabak, who patiently guided me through this project in all its details. I wish to thank Elana Attia, Rabbi and Mrs. Uri Kaploun, Yonadav Kaploun, Rabbi and Mrs. Shimon Rosen, Leibish and Sarah Hecht, and Rabbi Dovid Shapiro, who provided valuable comments after reviewing parts of the original manuscript. In addition, I am grateful to my friends **Fred Black**, Dr. Zvi Dwolatzky, Rivka Epstein, Dr. Menachem Gross, Tuvia Heller, Louise and Stuart Levine, Zvi Marsh, Bernie and Joyce Nappen, and Moshe Stern for their support.

I want to express my deepest gratitude to my dear uncle, Dr. Burton F. Jaffe, M.D., Boston, Massachusetts, for his contribution in memory of his late parents, my late grandparents, Irving and Lillian Jaffe, may their memories be a blessing to us all.

Thanks to my dear friends, Professor Leon Epstein, of Hadassah Medical School, and his wife, Aviva Epstein, past president of the Israel Dietetic Association, for their consistent encouragement and invaluable professional advice.

Warmest thanks to the entire Feldheim staff, especially to Rivka Mishmor, who saved me with her meticulous copyediting, and to Harvey Klineman, art director. Thanks to my typesetter Hannah Hartman and to proofreader Dvora Rhein. Special thanks to Ben Gasner for a truly magnificent cover design. My deepest appreciation to Mr. Yaakov Feldheim, who enabled me to turn my dream into a reality.

Preface

"You are what you eat." Let's expand this well-known expression and consider, "You are what and *the way* you eat."

Our eating style reflects and affects who and what we are. It identifies our approach to life. If we examine various societies and cultures, we see that each has its traditional foods and food ceremonies. "I am Italian. I often eat spaghetti, lasagna, or pizza"; "I am a real American. I eat hamburgers, hot dogs, steak, coke, and french fries." The French eat crepes, Belgians eat waffles, Chinese eat rice, Ethiopians eat teff, the Swiss eat chocolate, Israelis eat felafel, and Eskimos eat whale blubber. In short, the "way we eat" reveals how we identify ourselves. It reflects and often determines our world-view, our values, and our entire approach to life.

"You are the way you eat." Foods are much more than just a collection of nutrients; they are a wealth of influences and connotations. Rare foods and spices are treasured as special culinary delights. Some foods are worshiped in various cultures as having an unusual holiness or are avoided altogether. The type of food we choose can affect our moods. Hot, spicy, or stimulating foods may influence many of us toward hot-temperedness or nervousness. Cooling foods can relax us and give us peace of mind. Foods can help us celebrate and can comfort us when we mourn. They are a sign of love and are a means of uniting people on many occasions.

The various religions use foods to connote their special approach to life. When taken to an extreme, the foods themselves can become the main ritual and one can lose all perspective. Foods may even be worshiped as all-powerful and as the giver of life. This approach to eating is not the Jewish way.

What is your identity? Remember, the "way you eat" (and dress and speak) reveals how you identify yourself. As a Jew, you do not have to imitate others to obtain your identity. Instead, examine your own special, ancient Jewish roots.

We, as Jews, have special God-given food habits followed faithfully by most Jews for thousands of years. This food system is based on the rules of kashrus, with a separation of milk- and meat-containing foods. There are many other special details involved in our system of eating which I shall not discuss here (*shechitah*, Shabbos, Pesach, *terumah*, *ma'aser*, *orlah*, etc.).

The "way we eat" as Jews is an important part of our heritage and spans from simple rules of common eating etiquette to complex kabbalistic combinations of God's Divine Name (*kavannos*) concentrated upon while eating. We make a blessing over our food before and after eating and thank God for His wonderful kindness which enables us to eat and to continue our lives for His service.

Traditional Jewish dishes have developed which have many important cultural and religious connotations. Nevertheless, those of us choosing to follow a healthier, lighter style of eating can find a firm foundation for natural nutrition in the 800-year-old writings of the Rambam, Rabbi Moshe ben Maimon, the great Torah scholar and physician. One of the foremost preventive-health advocates of all time, the Rambam prescribes a synthesis of good health and a nutritional lifestyle reflecting and deepening our connection to our own Jewish roots.

It is with this orientation that I have developed my own approach to natural nutrition, striving to combine a system for healthy living and eating with a strong connection to our important Jewish heritage. I only pray that, with Hashem's help, I have been successful.

Yaakov Levinson
Jerusalem, 5755 (1995)

Introduction
Jewish Roots for Natural Nutrition

Rabbi Moshe ben Maimon (known by the acronym the RAMBAM, and also as Maimonides) was born in Cordova, Spain, in 4894 (1135). Due to religious persecution, he moved first to southern Spain and then to Fez, Morocco, where he studied medicine with such famous physicians as Ibn Zuhr and Abu Yusuf. At age thirty he left for Egypt, where he lived for the remaining thirty-nine years of his life. The Rambam wrote ten medical works, but he was especially esteemed as one of the greatest Torah authorities of all times. His expertise and writings included all areas of Jewish law and philosophy. He passed away in 4964 (1204) in Cairo and was laid to rest in Tiberias, Israel, after an illustrious, prolific religious and medical career.

The Rambam's medical writings contain the Jewish roots of today's system of natural nutrition. Our modern approach is basically an extension of his main principles and teachings. He emphasized the importance of preventive medicine and disease prevention. He foreshadowed today's "discovery" of the effect of proper lifestyle, discussing the role of diet and exercise. Mind-body interaction was primary in his approach to illness and wellness.

His medical writings were based on Jewish Talmudic sources as well as on secular, non-Jewish teachings. The Rambam wrote that all our actions should be only for the sake of God. We cannot live without eating or drinking. Nevertheless, we should eat and drink with the intention of preserving the health of our bodies. To achieve this aim the Rambam advocated eating health-giving foods and the avoidance of eating as a response to purely animalistic desires. He considered efforts to ensure a healthy body the way of Godliness and not separate from Judaism. He also added that we should avoid those practices that weaken and destroy our bodies.

To preserve health the Rambam taught that we should eat only when genuinely hungry and drink when truly thirsty. Drinking during meals should be minimized to avoid diluting the digestive juices. The preservation of good health rests on the avoidance of overeating, which he refers to as "the poison of death" and the cause of most illness. He taught us that eating a little of bad foods is actually less harmful than eating a lot of good and healthy food.

He advocated some exercise before eating to warm the body for improved digestion, and in general taught that exercise removes the harm caused by most bad habits which most people have. Meals should be eaten while sitting or reclining, and we should rest after meals for good digestion. Avoidance of constipation is essential for good health. Eating according to the seasons was also promoted, with cool foods and lesser quantities in the summer and warm, spicier foods in greater quantities in the winter.

Whole-grain bread was cited by the Rambam as "the best of food." The bread must not be made of refined flour and should consist of the rough grain, unchaffed and unpolished. He taught that white bread or bread made of refined flour was not a good food.

Poultry is promoted over red meat as lighter and more rapidly digested. All heavy, fatty meats are called "bad." Fatty cheeses, as well, are listed as "bad" foods; fresh, low-fat cheeses are recommended.

The Rambam cautions us against overeating fruits. On the other hand, he says that figs, grapes, and almonds are always good, and we know these are rich in nutrients. Unripe fruits, he claims, are like swords to the body and should be avoided.

The Rambam, in short, stressed that most illness results from eating bad foods or from overeating, even good foods. These teachings are, therefore, our Jewish roots for natural nutrition.

Part I:
The Nutrients

Since maintaining a healthy and sound body is among the ways of God — for one cannot understand or have any knowledge of the Creator, if he is ill — therefore, one must avoid that which harms the body and accustom himself to that which is healthful and helps the body become stronger.

      RAMBAM, Mishneh Torah, Book of Knowledge 4:1

Our Rabbis, of blessed memory, said (Berachos 63a): "Which is a short verse upon which all the principles of the Torah depend? It is (Mishlei 3:6): 'In all thy ways acknowledge Him.' This means that in all our actions, even those which we must do in order to sustain life, we must acknowledge the Lord, and do them for the sake of His Name, blessed be He. For instance, eating, drinking...."

      Shulchan Aruch 31:1

*And your threshing shall reach to the vintage,
and the vintage shall reach to the sowing time:
and you shall eat your bread to the full,
and dwell in your land safely.*

VAYIKRA 26:5

1 | The nutrients and their importance

Our food contains 40 to 45 substances known as "nutrients" which each of us must consume in adequate amounts in order to grow and to lead a healthy life. These nutrients enter our bodies from the food we eat and are converted into thousands of essential substances necessary for life! Nutrients therefore nourish the body.

Nutritionists speak of six general classes of nutrients, listed as follows:

> Carbohydrates   Fats   Proteins
> Vitamins   Minerals   Water

Since food is so vital to life, as described by the famous saying "You are what you eat," one should really know about the nutritive content of foods. One needs to know which ones are the best sources of the various nutrients and how to combine them into a healthful, balanced diet.

CARBOHYDRATES

Carbohydrates are used in the body as a source of energy and supply 4 calories per 0.035 oz.(1 g.). People generally need a minimum of 3.5 oz.(100 g.) of carbohydrate daily to maintain good health. Food sources of carbohydrate include cereals, potatoes, beans, corn, bread, and sugars.

FATS

Calories, whether from dietary carbohydrate or fat, are principally stored in the body as fat in the fat cells. Fat is the most concentrated source of energy, providing more than twice the number of calories than does either protein or carbohydrate. To be more exact, fat supplies 9 calories per 0.035 oz.(1 g.). Fat acts as a carrier for the fat-soluble vitamins A, D, E, and K. Fat deposits also insulate and cushion the body. Food sources of fat include oils, margarine, and butter.

PROTEINS
Protein is the major structural component of every cell in the body. Protein is the main constituent of muscle, nerves, skin, hair, and nails, as well as being a part of hormones and enzymes. Protein may be used for energy if necessary (4 calories per 0.035 oz.[1 g.]), and it is essential for the repair of tissues. In combination with iron, it forms hemoglobin in the blood. Food sources of protein include meat, poultry, fish, beans and peas, eggs, cheese, milk, and milk products.

VITAMINS
Vitamins are organic compounds required by the body from outside in very small amounts. They have a specific function in the regulation of body processes. Vitamins are normally supplied to our bodies by the food we eat. Persons following restrictive diets or having certain illnesses may require vitamin supplements as well.

Vitamins are generally divided into two major groups as shown in the table on page 13.

MINERALS
Minerals are inorganic (non-carbon containing) nutrients which have definite demonstrable functions in the human body and metabolism. Although minerals constitute only a small portion of the body (about 4%), they are essential as structural elements and in many vital processes.

Minerals are often classed as either macro- or micronutrients, depending on the amount of each that is needed in the diet. The charts on page 13 show this division.

WATER
Water comprises the largest single compound of total body

weight. Persons must maintain a fluid balance, avoiding dehydration, which may usually be achieved by an intake of 6 to 8 cups of fluid per day.

Certain medical conditions increase the body's need for water, such as fever, hot and dry environment, injury and burns, and uncontrolled diabetes mellitus.

In conditions where fluid retention occurs (chronic renal failure, congestive heart failure, liver disease), fluid restriction may be necessary.

Vitamins	
FAT-SOLUBLE	WATER-SOLUBLE
Vitamin A	Vitamin C (ascorbic acid)
Vitamin D	Vitamin B_1 (thiamin)
Vitamin E	Vitamin B_2 (riboflavin)
Vitamin K	Niacin
	Vitamin B_6 (pyridoxine)
	Vitamin B_{12}
	Pantothenic acid
	Folacin (folic acid)
	Biotin

Minerals			
MACROMINERALS		MICROMINERALS	
Calcium	Phosphorus	Zinc	Chromium
Iron	Sodium	Iodine	Copper
Potassium	Chlorine	Manganese	Fluorine
Magnesium	Sulfur	Molybdenum	Cobalt
		Selenium	Nickel
		Tin	Vanadium
		Silicon	

It shall even be as when a hungry man dreams, and, behold, he eats....

YESHAYAHU 29:8

2 | Weight = energy
(A few words on desirable weight)

Overeating is like poison to anyone's body. It is the main source of all illness. Most illnesses which afflict a man are caused by harmful foods or by his filling his belly and overeating, even of healthful foods.

This was implied by Shelomo in his wisdom: Whoever guards his mouth and his tongue, guards his soul from distress (*Mishlei* 21:23), i.e., "guards his mouth" from eating harmful food or eating his fill and "his tongue" from speaking [about things] other than his needs.

Rambam, *Mishneh Torah, Book of Knowledge* 4:15

One should not eat until his stomach is full. Rather, he should stop when he is close to three-quarters of full satisfaction.

Rambam, *Mishneh Torah, Book of Knowledge* 4:2

Therefore, we must not eat whatever is palatable just like the dog and the donkey do, but we should eat only the things that are helpful to, and good for, the health of the body. There are some saintly people who, before partaking of food or drink, say: "I am ready to eat and drink in order that I may gain health and strength to worship the Creator, blessed be His Name."

Shulchan Aruch 31:2

Why not be overweight?

Ask any overweight person what it means to be obese. Needless to say, there are aesthetic reasons why the overweight person would love to wake up in the morning twenty pounds lighter! Constant embarrassment and self-consciousness about one's "weight problem" are difficult to cope with on a regular basis. The need for special clothing of extra-large sizes is certainly no advantage. The social implications for the child, adolescent, or young adult wishing to marry are many and complex. The husband-wife and other adult interpersonal relationships are often strained due to unwanted extra baggage in societies where being trim is admired and being overweight is viewed as unattractive, if not abhorrent!

Besides the cosmetic and social implications, which seem to be the main concerns of most obese persons, there are, as well, the health hazards of obesity which should be of even greater concern as they are often life-threatening!

Obesity is the major nutrition-related problem in most developed societies. With all of the efforts exerted on an individual basis, as well as much research into the cause and treatment of obesity, there is nothing to indicate that the overall incidence of obesity is declining. In fact, the opposite appears to be true, with increasing levels of obesity corresponding to increasing national affluence. Most overweight people, contrary to popular opinion, do try to correct their weight problem. They try and try again; but in the great majority of cases the lost weight returns and is usually accompanied by an additional weight gain as soon as the discipline is relaxed.

Investigation has shown that obesity is certainly a factor in shortening the life span and in the increased incidence of common illnesses — diabetes, heart disease and vascular disorders such as atherosclerosis, coronary artery disease, high blood pressure, and gallbladder disease, as well as orthopedic problems.

Studies in the United States have shown that obesity is clearly a factor contributing to increased risk of developing three of the four major health problems (heart disease, high blood pressure, and diabetes) and is probably a factor in the development of the fourth (cancer). Furthermore, complications are more common in the obese during acute illness and following accidents, general anesthesia, and surgery.

Contrary to popular belief, endocrine (hormone) disorders only rarely cause increased appetite or decreased metabolic rates and obesity. In addition, research has indicated that overfeeding in early childhood can increase the number of fat cells, that is, the amount of fat in the body; and a fat child may therefore be prepared for suffering from a weight problem for the rest of his life.

When is a person considered overweight?

"Overweight" is weight greater than normal as compared with standard height and weight tables (with adjustments for sex and body frame variations). This refers to excess weight of every component of the body, including bone and muscle, as well as fat.

"Obesity" refers only to abnormal amounts of body fat. "Overweight" and "obesity" are not always identical; an overweight person may not necessarily be obese, with excess fat stores. In the usual cases, practically speaking, most persons may be considered "obese" when they become 15-20% overweight, as compared to a standard table of heights and weights, such as follows:

Desirable Weights for Adults

HEIGHT (without shoes)	WEIGHT IN POUNDS (without clothing)	
	MEN	WOMEN
4'8"	—	96-107
4'10"	—	101-113
5'0"	—	107-119
5'2"	121-133	113-126
5'4"	127-139	120-135
5'6"	134-147	128-143
5'8"	142-156	136-151
5'10"	150-165	144-159
6'0"	158-175	—

For measurements according to frame size, see Appendix 1, "About calories."

A more direct method to determine body fat is that of measuring a fold of skin on the back of the arm with special calipers. Minimum measurements of 7/8 in. (23 mm.) for males and 13/16 in. (30 mm.) for females are used as guidelines for defining obesity.

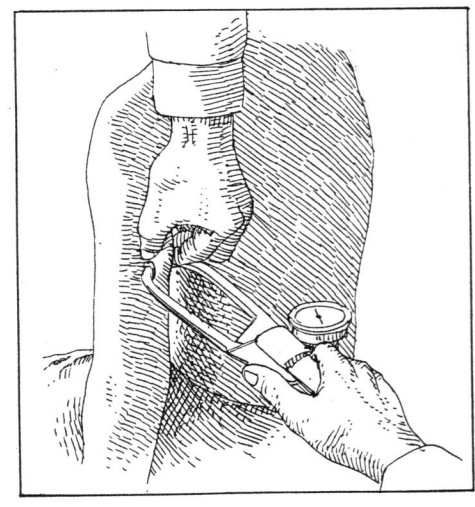

Previous attempts to treat obesity: frustrations and hazards

Several popular approaches constantly present themselves in a repetitive cycle throughout the years as "new solutions" to the obesity problem. The following is a discussion of some of the recent "favorites," which range anywhere from frustrating time-wasters to short-term successes to life-threatening menaces! At times, the only weight loss is due to a severe lightening of the cash content of the patient's pocket. A brief discussion of these topics should be informative or at least amusing.

TOTAL FASTING is a weight-reduction technique employed from ancient times. Generally, the subject has hunger cravings for 48 to 72 hours, after which he experiences no particular hunger. However, psychological as well as physical complaints often accompany this method, including liver dysfunction, infection, cardiac complications, and high levels of uric acid. Moreover, most weight losses with this method are not of fat but rather of protein and fluid, which is a most undesirable result.

A PROTEIN-SPARING DIET of 600 calories or less per day, consisting only of liquid proteins or of proteins from food sources as well as vitamins and minerals, was quite popular until several deaths due to cardiac arrhythmias were reported in the United States and Canada among persons following this severe diet even while they were under a physician's care. Many complaints of illness have also occurred.

LIQUID DIETS generally consist of a "complete food" in package form or in cans which supplies the dieter with his total daily food intake. No solid food is taken. Several dangerous side effects have been reported, such as hyperuricemia (excess uric acid in the blood) and hypotension (low blood pressure).

LOW-CARBOHYDRATE DIETS of several variations have circulated. The diets are extremely low in carbohydrate (bread and starches, fruits and vegetables) and extremely high in protein and in fat (fatty meats and cheese). These diets are "effective" only to the extent that fewer calories are consumed and have nothing to do with specifically eliminating all carbohydrates.

There is no reason to associate a diet rich in carbohydrate with obesity. Also, there are many potential hazards of a diet very low in carbohydrate and rich in fat. The greatest danger due to the high fat content of the diet over long periods of time is the development of hyperlipidemia (excessive fat in the blood), which may consist of cholesterol or of triglycerides. This is associated with an increased risk of developing coronary heart disease, as well as another vascular disease called atherosclerosis, with accompanying fat deposits on the walls of the veins. Other possible complications include increases in blood uric acid with the disease called gout, extreme fatigue, and low blood pressure.

If a person is willing to torture himself for enough time on this regime (as on many of the other "diets" discussed in this section), he will probably lose weight temporarily despite the inconvenience, but he will run the risk of developing the many harmful side effects of the "diet" as well.

Many diets generally low in calories are floating around, some better designed than others, and these generally fall into the hands of the veteran dieter. These STANDARD PRINTED DIETS are at times nutritionally balanced and even occasionally add up to the caloric content claimed by the diet's author on the printed sheets! Needless to say, these are never individualized to meet the specific dieter's needs or food likes and dislikes. The classic picture is that of one who hates cottage cheese forcing platefuls down his throat five times a day — with dreams of one day being slim and trim — and hating every minute of it.

A discussion of food restriction to produce weight loss would be incomplete without mentioning the many "WONDER FOODS" often recommended as miraculous "cures" to burn off unwanted fat. I should think that the monotony of these diets alone would drive one away from the struggle of weight reduction. For example, one such diet involves twelve days of consuming nothing but grapes, another only grapefruit, and still another only watermelon. Among the advocates of these diets themselves there seems to be a large battle over which single food holds the key to a new thin life. Long-term success is never produced.

The medical profession also has entered the arena of weight reduction with modern TECHNOLOGICAL "SOLUTIONS" to the weight problem. These, as well, range from harmless to life-threatening! Hormonal disorder, which is now known rarely to be a cause of obesity, has often been promoted. Pills to reduce appetite are often prescribed. The effect of these medications generally lasts only 4 to 6 weeks, and they may be associated with significant difficulties, including severe paranoid psychological reactions and addiction. The artificial bulk-producing agents (stomach fillers) prescribed are generally not helpful.

Several SURGICAL APPROACHES have been widely advocated with often questionable results and associated risks. Intestinal bypass is a procedure in which a portion of the intestine is removed, thereby creating a shorter intestinal tract. The operation may produce lasting weight loss for some, but such surgery also has a high frequency of serious complications. One study reports the death of 3% of patients operated on. Another source quotes a mortality rate of 9%. Apparently this does not discourage many desperate overweight persons from risking their lives in order to perhaps escape the curse of eternal obesity.

A major problem of the surgery is the subsequent development of diarrhea and nutrient malabsorption, whereby food eaten is not actually absorbed into the body, and the person may thereby develop severe nutrient deficiencies (such as of potassium, calcium, and magnesium). Also, some patients develop severe liver damage, intestinal inflammation, or renal problems. In many cases the body adjusts to the shortened intestine, and the patient returns to his original weight despite all the agony he has experienced. In short, the risks involved hardly make it worthwhile for most people to take a chance on this approach.

JAW WIRING is another surgical approach that is sometimes used, making it impossible for the patient to significantly open his mouth. The patient's dietary intake is reduced to a liquid diet taken through a straw. How pleasant this must be!

Several PSYCHOLOGICAL APPROACHES have been employed with varying success. Group pressure sessions may be quite successful with selected persons requiring mild weight reduction. The patient reduces his food intake, not wishing to appear unsuccessful before others who are also dieting. However, even the successful dieter generally returns to his previous weight when he stops attending the group sessions.

Psychiatric counseling and HYPNOSIS have also been employed to attempt to achieve weight reduction. Psychiatric treatment may produce good results if the patient has a treatable psychiatric disorder with obesity as a recent problem.

BEHAVIOR MODIFICATION, a psychological approach involving the replacement of undesirable behavior with more acceptable eating habits, has recently produced much success, especially when used in combination with diet therapy and exercise.

Programs of increased EXERCISE are also promoted to produce weight loss. Exercise bikes, reducing machines, and massage are now standardly used in the fight against obesity.

Recent success in weight reduction

Unfortunately, as one can see from the discussion just presented, a quick and easy cure for overeating has not yet been discovered. However, with the present understanding of principles of nutrition, combined with a careful approach in rearranging an overweight person's eating environment (known as behavior modification) as well as a program of exercise and of relaxation, we can now present hope in a high percentage of cases for moderate to good success on a long-term basis. This previously was not the case in the area of weight control, which is our number one nutrition problem. It is now known that a good reducing diet is one on which the patient does not become too hungry. To ensure success the diet must be individually designed by an experienced, qualified nutritionist or dietitian. Standardized diets on printed sheets are generally of no value. The patient's special needs must be recognized, and food likes and dislikes must be taken into account.

The patient's eating behavior must also be modified to replace habits which produce overeating with practices encouraging reduced food intake. It should be emphasized that the patient himself is not guilty. It is stressed to the patient that he has a tendency to become overweight, and that his surroundings make it too easy for him to overeat. Then, changes are made slowly to establish new desirable patterns of eating.

The Rambam wrote that exercise removes the harm caused by most bad habits which most people have. The main principle of exercise is that it is a movement that is vigorous and increases breathing. Modern researchers have shown that moderate exercise causes people actually to eat less. Furthermore, increased exercise increases the amount of calories burned or, in other words, helps to achieve added weight loss.

It must be repeatedly stressed that all changes in the person's eating or behavior patterns must be individually tailored to meet the patient's needs in order to ensure successful long-term weight reduction.

I recently treated a patient who well illustrates this point. In this spirit I was forced to calculate a diet that included five pieces of cake per week, two sticks of chewing gum per day, and sugar in tea. The patient reports not feeling especially hungry while following this otherwise low-calorie diet (1,200 calories daily, including cake, gum, and sugar) designed as closely as possible to suit her wishes regarding eating patterns and food choices, and to meet my standards of an overall healthy diet. The few permitted leniencies remove the pressure, allowing her to follow an otherwise restricted diet. In short, the patient conscientiously made all requested behavior changes with high rates of success, followed her diet carefully, and lost 18 pounds in four weeks!

Activity and Energy Expenditure

ACTIVITY	ENERGY EXPENDITURE
Light housework such as polishing furniture or washing small clothes Strolling 1 mile/hour	2-2.5 calories/minute
Walking 2 miles/hour	2.5-4 calories/minute
Cleaning windows, mopping floors Walking 3 miles/hour Cycling 6 miles/hour Ironing	4-5 calories/minute
Scrubbing floors Walking 4 miles/hour Cycling 8 miles/hour Stair climbing (at weight of 140 pounds)	5-6 calories/minute
Stair climbing (at weight of 180 pounds)	9 calories/minute
Swimming	5-11 calories/minute
Dancing	10 calories/minute
Running 5 miles/hour	10-11 calories/minute

Summation of Obesity "Cures" — Old and New

FASTING
  Total starvation

LIQUID DIETS
  Semi-starvation
  Protein-sparing diets
  Liquid-protein diets
  Liquid-formula diets (package or can)

ALTERATION OF USUAL DIETARY COMPOSITION
  Low-carbohydrate diets (ketogenic diets)
  Low-calorie diets
  Very-low-calorie diets
  Protein-sparing diets

SINGLE-FOOD CURES
  Grape diet
  Grapefruit diet
  Watermelon diet
  Seaweed (kelp) diet
  Rice diet
  Dietary additions: apple cider vinegar, bran, garlic, etc.

DRUGS AND SURGICAL PROCEDURES
  Correction of hormone abnormality
  Amphetamines (appetite-depressing drugs)
  Bulk producers (stomach fillers)
  Intestinal bypass, fat removal, jaw wiring
  Acupuncture

PSYCHOLOGICAL APPROACHES
  Psychiatric support
  Group pressure sessions
  Hypnosis
  Imagery training
  Diet meditation

EXERCISE APPROACHES
  Diet farms
  Massage
  Reducing machines

*...And wine that makes glad the heart of man;
oil to brighten his face;
and bread which sustains the heart of man.*

TEHILLIM 104:15

3 | Carbohydrates: source of energy

> Eighty-three illnesses are dependent on the gallbladder, and all of them are nullified by eating bread and drinking water in the morning.
> *Bava Metzia* 107b

> "Illness" has the numerical value of eighty-three.
> *Bava Kamma* 92b

> Morning bread saves one from: sun, cold, winds, harmful spirits.
> *Bava Metzia* 107b

> Eating morning bread makes one wise, meritorious in judgment, able to learn and teach Torah, and makes one's words heard.
> *Bava Metzia* 107b

What is the contribution of breads and cereals to the diet?

Cereals are seeds of the grass family. As a group, cereals contain approximately 75% carbohydrates, mainly starch and cellulose; 10% protein, which is mostly incomplete, that is, of lower quality than that of animal foods; also 1-2% fat; 10% water; and 1-2% vitamins and minerals. The most important cereals used for food are wheat, corn, rice, oats, rye, and barley. Cereal grains are used for making breads, various types of flour for baked goods (such as cakes and cookies), breakfast foods, pastas (such as spaghetti, macaroni, and noodles), and starches. Cereals are valuable mainly as an economic source of energy and are the major food in the diets of many people around the world.

Cereal grains can be separated into three different parts: bran, endosperm (starch storage), and germ.

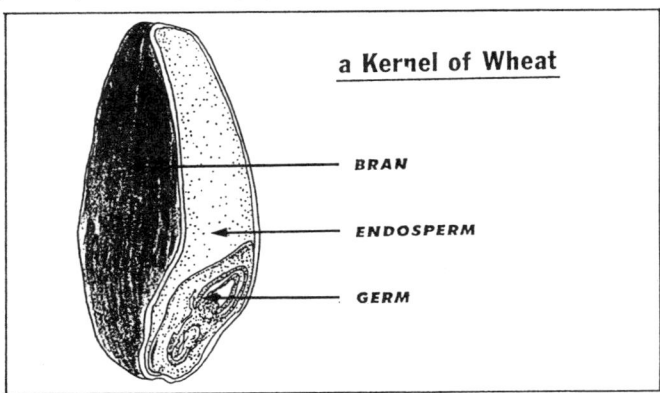

a Kernel of Wheat

BRAN
ENDOSPERM
GERM

The chaffy outermost coat that covers the kernel during growth is eliminated when the grains are harvested. The bran coat is the next outermost layer of the grain. This indigestible carbohydrate of cellulose comprises 5% of the entire grain. Bran is a source of fiber, iron, B-vitamins, and protein. The germ, comprising 2-3% of a cereal grain, is rich in unsaturated fat, protein, iron, and B-vitamins. The starchy endosperm, which is the major portion of the cereal grain, comprising 83% of the kernel, contains most of the kernel's starch and protein but very little vitamins, minerals, or fiber and only a trace of fat.

Cereals and their composition

Cereal products differ in composition and in nutritional value, depending upon the part of the grain used. All cereals furnish mainly starch and protein, but refined cereals, where the bran and the germ have been removed during processing, provide very little more! Whole-grain products, on the other hand, contain more vitamins and minerals than do refined products and are particularly valuable as dietary sources of iron, phosphorus, and thiamin. The laxative property of whole-grain cereals is due mainly to the fiber and components of the bran as well as, in part, to the oil of the germ.

What is fiber and why is it important?

Fiber has been a largely neglected component of food, mainly because it contributes little nutritionally. It has no calories and has scarcely any nutritional value. On the other hand, many of the diseases of our civilization have appeared only in the last century, and this may be due at least in part to the removal of fiber from the carbohydrate foods that constitute the major part of our diet!

Fiber may be defined as the indigestible carbohydrate comprising the outer coat of grains and cereals as well as the skins of fruits and vegetables. Fiber provides bulk in the diet and aids in elimination. It has, as well, an effect on the chemical and bacteriological processes that take place in the intestine.

Does lack of fiber in the diet cause disease?

Much evidence today would confirm that lack of fiber does cause disease. Diets high in cereal fibers are known to reduce symptoms of diverticulosis, a disease of the large intestines. High-fiber diets have also been used to lower blood cholesterol levels and to help control diabetes in those diabetics with normal digestive function.

Some researchers have also claimed a connection between diets lacking fiber and heart disease, appendicitis, gallbladder disease, varicose veins, deep vein thrombosis, hiatus hernia, hemorrhoids, and cancer of the colon. The laxative effect of fiber would theoretically support these claims in diseases known to arise from chronic constipation and straining on elimination.

In recommending an ideal fiber intake, one must consider the possible deleterious effects of a diet low in fiber as opposed to possible nutrient malabsorption caused by extremely high-fiber diets. Therefore, nutritionists recommend a moderate increase in dietary fiber consumption, achievable by increased intake of whole-grain cereal products, vegetables, and fruit.

Dietary Fiber in Foods

Food	Quantity	Fiber (grams)
FRUITS		
Apple (with skin)	1 medium	3.5
Banana	1 medium	2.4
Cantaloupe	1/4 melon	1.0
Cherries	10	1.2
Orange	1 medium	2.6
Peach (with skin)	1	1.9
Pear (with skin)	1/2 large	3.1
Prunes	3	3.0
Raisins	1/4 cup	3.1
Raspberries	1/2 cup	3.1
Strawberries	1 cup	3.0
VEGETABLES, COOKED		
Asparagus	1/2 cup	1.0
Beans, string	1/2 cup	1.6
Broccoli	1/2 cup	2.2
Brussels sprouts	1/2 cup	2.3
Parsnips	1/2 cup	2.7
Potato (with skin)	1 medium	2.5
Spinach	1/2 cup	2.1
Sweet potato	1/2 medium	1.7

Turnip	1/2 cup	1.6
Zucchini	1/2 cup	1.8
VEGETABLES, RAW		
Celery, diced	1/2 cup	1.1
Cucumber	1/2 cup	0.4
Lettuce	1 cup	0.9
Mushrooms, sliced	1/2 cup	1.5
Spinach	1 cup	1.2
Tomato	1 medium	1.5
LEGUMES		
Baked beans	1/2 cup	8.8
Dried peas, cooked	1/2 cup	4.7
Kidney beans, cooked	1/2 cup	7.3
Lentils, cooked	1/2 cup	3.7
Lima beans, cooked	1/2 cup	4.5
Navy beans, cooked	1/2 cup	6.0
BREADS AND CEREALS		
Bran muffins	1 muffin	2.5
Cornflakes	1 1/4 cup	0.3
French bread	1 slice	0.7
Oatmeal, cooked	3/4 cup	1.6
Pumpernickel bread	1 slice	1.0
Rice, brown, cooked	1/2 cup	1.0
Spaghetti, cooked	1/2 cup	1.1
Whole-wheat bread	1 slice	1.4
NUTS AND SEEDS		
Almonds	10 nuts	1.1
Peanuts	10 nuts	1.4
Popcorn, popped	1 cup	1.0

What is the nutritional content of matzah vs. bread?

The Rambam considered matzah a bad food, to be eaten only in very small amounts and not to be eaten at all during the summer. I would attribute this to its constipating effect, which the Rambam himself repeatedly mentions in his writings as an unhealthy situation.

Nutritionally, matzah contains one-fourth the water of bread and 30% more calories per equivalent serving. There are roughly equal amounts of protein. On the other hand, matzah has 40% more carbohydrate but 73% less fat than bread. Matzah has only a trace of salt (sodium), with almost no vitamins or minerals. Whole-grain bread, in contrast, has small amounts of the B-vitamins as well as iron and fiber.

In short, matzah is low in salt, low in fat, and low in water, and equivalent to bread in its protein content. On the other hand, it is higher in calories and lacks vitamins, minerals, and fiber.

	Matzah 1 piece	White bread 1 slice	Whole-wheat bread 1 slice
weight	1.1 oz.	0.85 oz.	0.88 oz.
protein	3.0 g.	2.0 g.	2.4 g.
carbohydrates	25.4 g.	11.7 g.	11.4 g.
fat	0.3 g.	0.9 g.	1.1 g.
calories	117	64	61

What is the difference between white rice and brown rice?

Whole rice (brown with the husks) and white rice (hulled) are calorically equivalent. Both contain protein, amino acids, carbohydrate, fat, and potassium.

The advantage of whole rice over white rice is in the amount of fiber, B-vitamins, iron, and other minerals that it contains. All these are important to a person who relies on rice as a main component of his diet. However in those areas where rice is not eaten regularly as a main food but, rather, serves as a side dish, once or twice a week, there is no significant nutritional advantage to brown rice.

A disadvantage of whole rice is that it is difficult to store properly to prevent contamination by worms and insects. White rice, on the other hand, has a far longer and better storage capacity, due to the processing it has undergone.

It is important to note that, as rice undergoes the refining and whitening process, most of its vitamins and minerals are lost. Excessive consumption of white rice may cause constipation, especially in persons with limited fruit, vegetable, and fluid intake.

Whole rice is more expensive than white rice. Rice is imported from the Far East and must go through a long and difficult storage period until we actually obtain it. Whole rice is brought in smaller amounts, at more frequent intervals, which accounts for its higher price.

An additional disadvantage to whole rice is that it is very difficult to check for worms and insects. Its nutritional benefit in relation to white rice is not significant, as explained, when it is eaten in limited amounts and would not justify all the efforts sometimes required to check the whole rice properly. The minerals forfeited can easily be obtained through other food sources.

Is the potato fattening?

The "pure starch" myth about potatoes being fattening is far from justified! The potato is a fine contribution to the diet, providing a good source of vitamins (C, B-complex), minerals (iron, calcium, and phosphorus), essential carbohydrate, and small amounts of high-quality vegetable protein. Potatoes are low in sodium (important for those on low-salt diets), almost fat free, and easy to digest.

Potatoes grown in South America as early as 1,800 years ago

were probably a haphazard mixture of varieties. Considered by many to be native to the Peruvian-Bolivian Andes, the potato was encountered by the invading Spaniards and was subsequently introduced into Europe during the second half of the sixteenth century.

Potatoes may be prepared in many ways (boiled, steamed, mashed, roasted, baked, fried, and in kugels, latkes, or chulents) and can add variety as well as an important nutritional contribution to one's diet.

What does sugar provide to the body?

Sugars are essentially energy foods and in general do not supply other nutrients besides carbohydrates in significant amounts. As a rule, the more refined the sugar the more limited is its nutritive value.

For example, white sugar would have somewhat less nutritional value than brown sugar, though this would vary according to processing procedures. On comparison of sugar and honey, one finds approximately equal nutrient content, with each basically a source of calories in the form of carbohydrate. The exception is molasses, which is actually an excellent source of calcium and of iron.

Sugars are useful as fuel for the body, but in large amounts they may produce unwanted side effects. When overeaten, sugars cause a loss of appetite, decreasing the consumption of foods containing protein, vitamins, and minerals. Sugar in large amounts may have a disturbing and irritating effect on the digestive tract. Bacterial decomposition of sugars, before absorption in the intestine, may result in gas formation and in the production of irritating amounts of lactic acid and other fermentation products.

High sugar intakes combine with fats in the blood, which may lead to heart disease.

The overuse of sugars together with the neglect of other essential foods is a factor in the malnutrition of children and is

Carbohydrates: source of energy

also a causative factor in tooth decay.

1 tablespoon	Calories	Carbohydrate (g.)	Protein (g.)	Calcium (mg.)	Iron (mg.)
Sugar	46	11.9	0	0	0
Honey	61	16.5	0.1	1	0.1
Molasses	43	11	0	116	2.3

Hidden Sugars in Foods

Food	Quantity	Sugar (teaspoons)
BEVERAGES		
Cola drinks	6 fl. oz.	3 1/2
Ginger ale	6 fl. oz.	5
Orangeade	8 fl. oz.	5
Lemon-Lime	6 fl. oz.	3 3/4
CAKES AND COOKIES		
Angel food	4 oz. piece	7
Banana cake	4 oz. piece	4
Cheese cake	4 oz. piece	2
Chocolate cake (plain)	4 oz. piece	6
Chocolate cake (iced)	4 oz. piece	10
Coffee cake	4 oz. piece	4 1/2
Cupcake (iced)	1	6
Pound cake	4 oz. piece	5
Sponge cake	4 oz. piece	8
Brownies (unfrosted)	1 (3/4 oz.)	3
Chocolate cookies	1	1 1/2

Macaroons	1	6
Sugar cookies	1	1 1/2
Donut (glazed)	1	6

CANDIES

Chocolate bar (milk)	1 1/2 oz.	2 1/2
Chewing gum	1 stick	1/2
Fudge	1 oz. square	4 1/2
Gumdrop	1	2
Hard candy	4 oz.	20

CANNED FRUITS AND JUICES

Apricots, canned	4 halves and 1 tbsp. syrup	3 1/2
Fruit juices, sweet, canned	1/2 cup	2
Fruit salad	1/2 cup	3 1/2
Peaches, canned	2 halves and 1 tbsp. syrup	3 1/2

DAIRY PRODUCTS

Ice cream	1/3 pt.	3 1/2
Ice cream cone	1	3 1/2
Ice cream soda	1	5
Ice cream sundae	1	7
Malted milk shake	10 fl. oz.	5

JAMS AND JELLIES

Apple butter	1 tbsp.	1
Jelly	1 tbsp.	4-6

DESSERTS

Apple cobbler	1/2 cup	3
Custard	1/2 cup	2

Carbohydrates: source of energy

French pastry	4 oz. piece	5
Fruit gelatin	1/2 cup	4 1/2
Apple pie	1 slice	7
Berry pie	1 slice	10
Pumpkin pie	1 slice	5
Banana pudding	1/2 cup	2
Chocolate pudding	1/2 cup	4
Plain pastry	4 oz. piece	3
Sherbet	1/2 cup	9

SYRUPS, SUGARS AND ICINGS

Brown sugar	1 tbsp.	3
Chocolate icing	1 oz.	5
Chocolate sauce	1 tbsp.	3 1/2
Corn syrup	1 tbsp.	3
Honey	1 tbsp.	3
Maple syrup	1 tbsp.	5
Molasses	1 tbsp.	3 1/2
White icing	1 oz.	5

*One should guard oneself against
all things that are dangerous,
because "Regulations concerning health and life
are made more stringent than ritual laws"
(Chullin 10a);
and the risk of danger is to be apprehended
even more than the risk of infringing upon a precept.*

SHULCHAN ARUCH 33:7

4 | Fats: storehouse of energy

Are all fats and oils unhealthy?

Calories, whether from dietary carbohydrate or fat, are principally stored in the body as fat in the adipose cells. Fat is the most concentrated source of energy, providing more than twice the number of calories than does either protein or carbohydrate. Also, fat acts as a carrier for the fat-soluble vitamins A, D, E, and K.

Fat provides certain essential fatty acids — for example, linoleic acid, which the body cannot produce. Fats may be classified into three categories: polyunsaturated, monounsaturated, and saturated.

Saturated fats are usually solid at room temperature. Most are generally found in animal foods: milk products, meat, and chicken. But there are also some in vegetable fats, such as coconut oil. Unsaturated fats are usually liquid at room temperature. Most are found in vegetable foods, such as vegetable oils. These may be divided into monounsaturated and polyunsaturated.

The degree of saturation depends on the number of hydrogen atoms per molecule and is related to the chemical structure of the fat. The healthfulness of fats is related to the fat's influence on blood cholesterol levels, which are an important factor contributing to heart disease. As a rule, saturated fats tend to elevate blood cholesterol levels, while polyunsaturated and monounsaturated fats generally reduce blood cholesterol.

Kinds of Fats	
Fatty acid	*Examples*
Monounsaturated H H H H H H │ │ │ │ │ │ H–C–C–C=C–C–C–H │ │ │ │ H H H H	Avocado Cashews Olives Olive oil Peanut oil Peanuts
Polyunsaturated H H H H H H H │ │ │ │ │ │ │ H–C–C=C–C–C=C–C–H │ │ │ H H H	Almonds Corn oil Fish Mayonnaise Pecans Safflower oil Soybean oil Sunflower oil Walnuts
Saturated H H H H │ │ │ │ H–C–C–C–C–H │ │ │ │ H H H H	Butter Cheese Chocolate Coconut Egg yolk Meat Milk Palm oil Poultry Vegetable shortening

C carbon atom
H hydrogen atom
– single bond
= double bond

Cholesterol: a risk factor for heart disease

Cholesterol is a fat-like substance (lipid) which travels throughout the body in the blood. The cholesterol level in the blood is determined partly by heredity and partly by the fat and cholesterol content of the diet. Other factors, such as obesity and physical inactivity, appear also to contribute to a higher cholesterol. The majority of patients with coronary artery disease have an elevated blood cholesterol level. Blood cholesterol levels reflect one's dietary intake of cholesterol-containing foods.

A high blood cholesterol level is therefore one of the major risk factors associated with heart disease. Studies in the United States (Framingham, Massachusetts) have shown that a man with a blood cholesterol level of 250 or above has about three times the likelihood of suffering a heart attack compared with a man with a cholesterol level below 194. This data, as understood, must also be evaluated in conjunction with other major risk factors of heart disease (high blood pressure, smoking, overweight).

A high blood cholesterol level contributes to the development of atherosclerotic plaques that block arteries, which increases the risk of a heart attack.

The following chart shows values accepted as desirable, borderline, or high blood cholesterol:

Blood Cholesterol Level	
Less than 200 mg./dL	desirable blood cholesterol
200-239 mg./dL	borderline high
Greater than 240 mg./dL	high blood cholesterol

The American Academy of Pediatrics this year has urged physicians to test cholesterol levels in all children age 2 years and older who have a family history of high cholesterol or premature heart attack. Children with high cholesterol levels (176 mg. per 100 ml. of blood serum or higher) should be counseled on their diet by nutrition specialists.

More specifically, cholesterol may be divided into two types. One may speak of the "bad" LDL (low-density lipoprotein)-cholesterol, which sticks to artery walls and narrow passageways where blood needs to flow freely. On the other hand, the "good" HDL (high-density lipoprotein)-cholesterol helps prevent clogging of the arteries. Levels of LDL-cholesterol of 160 mg./dL or greater are classified as "high-risk LDL-cholesterol," and those of 130-159 mg./dL as "borderline-high-risk LDL-cholesterol." A low level of HDL-cholesterol (below 35 mg./dL) is considered another factor that will increase the overall risk of developing heart disease.

Nutrition advice for lowering blood cholesterol

Dietary therapy is considered the primary cholesterol-lowering treatment. Three dietary habits contribute to elevated blood cholesterol. First is a high intake of saturated fats. Second is a relatively high intake of cholesterol. Third is a high caloric intake that exceeds body requirements, commonly causing obesity.

As stated above, saturated fats as a rule tend to elevate blood cholesterol levels, causing an increased risk for the development of heart disease. On the other hand, polyunsaturated and monounsaturated fats tend to lower blood cholesterol levels.

In conclusion, the American Heart Association has recommended that:

1. no more than 30% of one's daily calories should be obtained from fat;

2. one-third of these fats, ideally, should be from polyunsaturated fatty acids, one-third from monounsaturated fatty acids, and one-third or less from saturated fatty acids;

3. one's intake of high-cholesterol foods should be reduced to not more than 300 mg. of cholesterol daily.

In short, it is advisable that one avoid too much fat, mainly saturated fat, and cholesterol-containing foods. Choose lean meat, fish, poultry, and beans and peas as protein sources. Use skim or low-fat milk and milk products. Moderate your use of egg yolks (three per week maximum) and organ meats. Limit the intake of fats and oils, especially those high in saturated fat, such as butter and cream and foods containing palm and coconut oils. Trim the fat off meats. Broil, bake, or boil rather than fry.

Does oil become more unhealthy as it is reused?

High temperatures such as those required for deep-fat frying can cause chemical changes in fat, converting the polyunsaturated to saturated, which, as explained, can have a blood-cholesterol-raising effect. In order to keep oil in its healthiest form, it is recommended that food not be cooked in oil for an excessive length of time and that the oil not be overheated or reused.

Cholesterol in Foods

Food	Quantity	Cholesterol (milligrams)
Beef (lean)	3 oz.	77
Butter	1 tbsp.	31
Cheese (25-30% fat)	3 oz.	77
Cheese, cream	3 oz.	108
Chicken, dark (no skin)	3 oz.	77
Chicken, white (no skin)	3 oz.	65
Cottage cheese	3 oz.	14
Egg white	1	0
Egg yolk	1	273
Fish, fresh	3 1/2 oz.	75
Frankfurter	2 (4 oz.)	112
Ice cream, vanilla	1 cup	59
Liver	3 oz.	270
Mayonnaise	1 tbsp.	8
Milk, skim	1 cup	5
Milk, whole	1 cup	34
Tuna, canned	3 oz.	55
Turkey, dark (no skin)	3 oz.	86
Yogurt, low-fat	1 cup	17

Fat in Foods

Food	Quantity	Fat (grams)
CANDY		
Fudge, chocolate	1 oz.	3.4
Hard candy	6 pieces	0.3
Milk chocolate	1 oz.	9.4
CHEESE PRODUCTS		
American	1 oz.	7.0
Swiss	1 oz.	6.8
CHIPS AND SNACKS		
Cheese twists	1 oz.	9.5
Corn chips	1 oz.	9.7
Popcorn	1 cup	0.7
Potato chips	10 pieces	8.0
Potato sticks	1 oz.	10.2
Pretzels	1 oz.	1.0
CREAMS		
Medium (25% fat)	1 tbsp.	3.8
Sour, cultured	1 tbsp.	2.5
Whipping, heavy	1 tbsp.	5.6
DESSERTS		
Brownies, chocolate	1	5.0
Cake		
Angel food	1 slice	0.1
Cheesecake	1 slice	16.3
Chocolate	1 slice	11.3
Cupcake	1	4.5

		Fat (grams)
Pound	1 slice	8.8
Sponge	1 slice	3.1
Custard	1/2 cup	7.3
Granola bar	1	4.2
Ice cream		
Chocolate	1 cup	16.0
Strawberry	1 cup	12.0
Vanilla, 10% fat	1 cup	14.3
Vanilla, 16% fat	1 cup	23.7
Ice milk, vanilla	1 cup	5.6
Ices, lime/orange	1 cup	trace
Popsicle	1 bar	0.0
Sherbet	1 cup	3.8
Yogurt, frozen	1/2 cup	1.0
PASTRY		
Cream puff	1	14.6
Danish pastry	1	4.9
Donut	1	8.0
Eclair	1	25.7
Pie		
Apple	1/8 pie	11.9
Banana cream	1/8 pie	12.0
Chocolate cream	1/8 pie	17.3
Coconut custard	1/8 pie	15.0
Pudding, instant	1/2 cup	4.7
Sweet roll	1	6.8
DESSERT TOPPINGS		
Butterscotch	2 tbsp.	7.2

Fats: storehouse of energy

		Fat (*grams*)
Chocolate fudge	2 tbsp.	3.8
Pineapple	3 tbsp.	0.2
EGGS		
Boiled	1 large	5.6
Fried	1 large	6.4
Scrambled, with milk & fat	1 large	7.1
White of egg	1	trace
Whole egg	1	5.6
Yolk	1	5.6
FATS, SHORTENING AND OILS		
Animal fats		
Butter	1 tbsp.	13.9
Chicken fat	1 tbsp.	12.8
Shortenings		
Soybean-cottonseed	1 tbsp.	12.8
Soybean-palm	1 tbsp.	12.8
Vegetable oils		
Corn oil	1 tbsp.	13.6
Olive oil	1 tbsp.	13.5
Peanut oil	1 tbsp.	13.5
Soybean oil	1 tbsp.	13.6
Sunflower oil	1 tbsp.	13.6
FISH		
Carp, raw	3 1/2 oz.	4.2
Herring, raw	3 1/2 oz.	11.3
Salmon	3 1/2 oz.	13.4
Sardines, in oil	4 medium	12.2

		Fat (grams)
Sardines, raw	3 1/2 oz.	8.6
Sole, raw	3 1/2 oz.	0.5
Tuna, albacore, in oil	6 1/2 oz.	19.9
Tuna, albacore, in water	6 1/2 oz.	3.5
Tuna, light, in oil	6 1/2 oz.	22.1
Tuna, light, in water	6 1/2 oz.	1.7
Whitefish, raw	3 1/2 oz.	8.2
GRAIN PRODUCTS		
Bagel	1	1.4
Bread		
Cracked wheat	1 slice	0.9
French	1 slice	1.0
Matzah	1 piece	0.3
Rye	1 slice	0.9
White	1 slice	0.9
Whole-wheat	1 slice	1.1
MEATS		
Beef		
Brisket, lean	3 slices	37.4
Chuck, lean	3 1/2 oz.	23.9
Corned beef	3 1/2 oz.	30.4
Hamburger	1 patty	14.5
Lamb		
Arm chop	3 1/2 oz.	27.0
Blade chop	3 1/2 oz.	26.1
Luncheon meats		
Bologna, beef	1 slice	6.5
Chicken roll	1 slice	2.1

Fats: storehouse of energy

		Fat (*grams*)
Frankfurter, beef	1	13.2
Salami, beef	1 slice	4.6
Turkey roll	1 slice	2.1
Organ meats		
Liver, beef, fried	3 1/2 oz.	10.6
Liver, beef, raw	3 1/2 oz.	3.8
Tongue, beef	3 1/2 oz.	16.7
MILK AND MILK PRODUCTS		
Milk, cow		
Low-fat, 1% fat	1 cup	2.6
Low-fat, 2% fat	1 cup	4.7
Skim	1 cup	0.4
Whole, 3.3% fat	1 cup	8.2
Milk, goat	1 cup	10.1
Milk, sheep	1 cup	17.2
Yogurt		
Plain, low-fat	1 cup	3.5
Plain, skim	1 cup	0.4
Plain, whole milk	1 cup	7.4
NUTS, NUT PRODUCTS & SEEDS		
Almond butter	1 oz.	9.1
Almonds	12-15 nuts	8.1
Brazil nuts	4 medium	9.9
Cashews, roasted	6-8 nuts	6.9
Chestnuts	3 small	0.2
Coconut, shredded	1/2 cup	16.3
Peanut butter	1 tbsp.	7.2
Peanuts, raw	30 nuts	13.2

		Fat (grams)
Pistachios	15 nuts	4.0
Seeds		
Pumpkin	1 oz.	13.1
Sesame	1 tbsp.	4.4
Sunflower	1 oz.	13.2
Soybean nuts	1 oz.	5.5
Walnuts, chopped	1 tbsp.	4.8
POULTRY		
Chicken		
Dark meat, no skin, fried	3 1/2 oz.	11.6
Dark meat, no skin, roasted	3 1/2 oz.	9.7
Dark meat, with skin, fried	3 1/2 oz.	16.9
Dark meat, with skin, roasted	3 1/2 oz.	15.8
Light meat, no skin, fried	3 1/2 oz.	5.5
Light meat, no skin, roasted	3 1/2 oz.	4.5
Light meat, with skin, fried	3 1/2 oz.	12.1
Light meat, with skin, roasted	3 1/2 oz.	10.9
Turkey		
Dark meat, no skin, roasted	3 1/2 oz.	7.2
Dark meat, with skin, roasted	3 1/2 oz.	11.5
Light meat, no skin, roasted	3 1/2 oz.	3.2
Light meat, with skin, roasted	3 1/2 oz.	8.3
SALAD DRESSINGS		
French	1 tbsp.	6.4
Italian	1 tbsp.	7.1
Russian	1 tbsp.	7.8
Sweet and sour	1 tbsp.	0.3

Fats: storehouse of energy

		Fat (grams)
SPREADS		
Butter	1 tbsp.	12.2
Cream cheese	1 tbsp.	5.3
Margarine	1 tbsp.	11.4
Mayonnaise	1 tbsp.	11.0

Food to a man is like oil to a lamp.
R. YEHUDA BEN HA-ROSH

זה המטרה ואהרן חתן שמן בנירות

5 | Protein: structure of the body

What is the importance of protein in the diet?

Protein is the major structural component of every cell in the body. It is the main constituent of muscle, nerves, skin, hair, and nails, as well as being a part of hormones and enzymes. Protein is necessary for the repair of tissues. In combination with iron, it forms hemoglobin in the blood. Proteins also may be used for energy if necessary, if carbohydrate and fats are not sufficient to meet energy needs. In short, one must have an adequate source of dietary protein to grow and to maintain oneself.

What are food sources of protein?

Are there differences in quantity and in quality of the various proteins?

Significant food sources of protein include meat, chicken, fish, dried beans and peas, nuts, eggs, cheese, milk, and milk products. Small amounts of protein are also contained in vegetables and in breads and cereals. Foods therefore vary widely in the amounts of protein that they contain.

Proteins consist of twenty-two or more nitrogen-containing compounds or units known as amino acids. Combinations and amounts of these units determine the degree of the protein's quality.

Amino acids which the body cannot form in adequate amounts are called "essential amino acids," since they must be supplied by the diet in proper proportions and amounts. Total protein intake along with adequate amounts of essential amino acids must be provided by the diet.

Differing amounts of the eight (in infants, nine) essential amino acids among various protein-containing foods determine the quality of protein available. When foods containing incomplete proteins are eaten, it is advisable to combine foods of complementary proteins to obtain all eight essential amino acids in optimal amounts by overlapping proteins from several food sources. For example, legumes should be combined with either grains or seeds and grains with milk products to ensure optimal protein quality.

Animal proteins, such as meat, chicken, fish, eggs, milk and milk products, provide good quality protein in good amounts. Plant proteins are usually not of as good quality and are incomplete.

The best quality plant proteins are in legumes, such as beans, peas, lentils, and peanuts, and in nuts.

The proteins in breads and cereals and in vegetables are incomplete. These are, nevertheless, significant as a part of the total protein intake when combined with other high-quality protein sources.

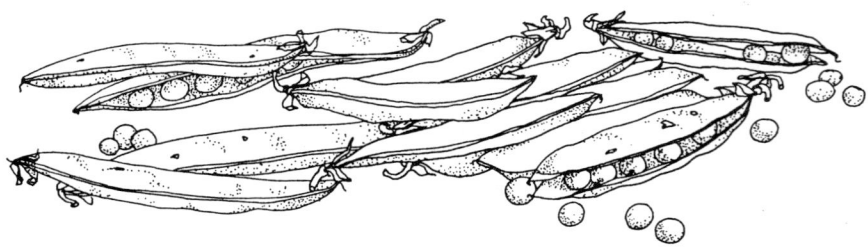

Protein in Foods

Food	Quantity	Protein (grams)
Almonds	12-15 nuts	2.8
Barley, dry	1 oz.	2.9
Beans, white, cooked	1/2 cup	7.8
Beef, chuck, cooked	3 oz.	22
Bread, white	1 slice	2
Bread, whole-wheat	1 slice	2.4
Buckwheat, dry	1 oz.	3
Bulgur, cooked	1 cup	8.4
Cheese, American	1 oz.	6.3
Cheese, cottage	1/2 cup	15.5
Chicken, no skin, roasted	3 oz.	25
Corn, kernels	1/2 cup	2.9
Egg	1	6.1
Fish, sole fillet	3 oz.	14
Lentils, cooked	2/3 cup	7.8
Macaroni, cooked	3/4 cup	3.6
Milk	1 cup	8
Oatmeal, dry	1 oz.	4.5
Peanut butter	1 tbsp.	3.9
Peanuts	1 oz.	7.5
Peas, green, cooked	2/3 cup	5.4
Potato, boiled	1 medium	1.9
Rice, brown, cooked	4/5 cup	3.8
Rice, white, cooked	4/5 cup	3
Sesame seeds	1 tbsp.	2.1
Soybeans, cooked	1/2 cup	11
Sunflower seeds, kernels	1 oz.	6.7
Sweet potato, baked	1 large	3.8

Tofu (soybean curd)	3 oz.	6.7
Tuna, in water	3 oz.	22
Turkey, no skin, roasted	3 oz.	25.6
Walnuts, chopped	1 tbsp.	1.1
Yogurt	1 cup	7.9

Can a vegetarian diet be healthy?

A vegetarian diet can definitely be set up in a healthy way, but a conscious effort is usually required to ensure optimal nutrition. In the ovo-lacto-vegetarian diet, protein is derived from animal and plant sources, including dairy products, eggs, cereals, legumes, nuts, and vegetables. Soy products may also be used.

In contrast, in the pure vegetarian diet protein is derived entirely from plant sources. There is a risk of inadequate protein intake due to a lack of essential amino acid proteins, with failure to overlap complementary proteins.

Furthermore, since vitamin B_{12} is not present in plant food, unless the pure vegetarian diet is supplemented with vitamin B_{12} it may, over several months or years, become life-threatening.

It is therefore recommended that persons who follow the strict "naturalist" vegetarian diet include liberal amounts of a variety of protein sources, such as grains, legumes, nuts, and vegetables. Vitamin B_{12} supplementation is considered essential.

The high-fiber, low-saturated-fat aspects of these diets, on the other hand, may be of great benefit in promoting good health.

Protein: structure of the body

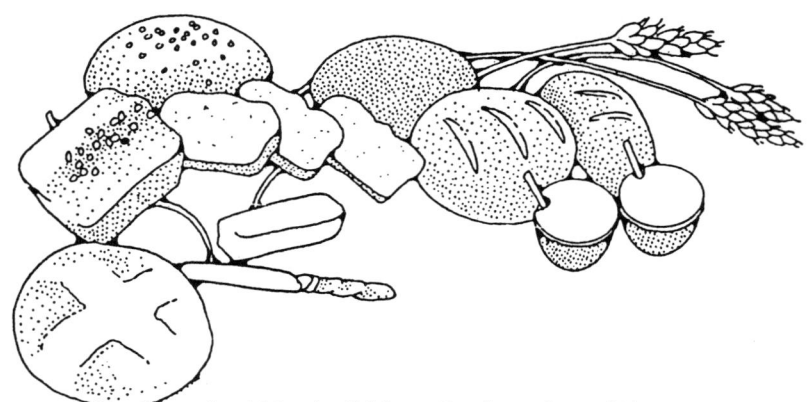

...And He shall bless thy bread, and thy water; and I will take sickness away from the midst of thee.

SHEMOS 23:25

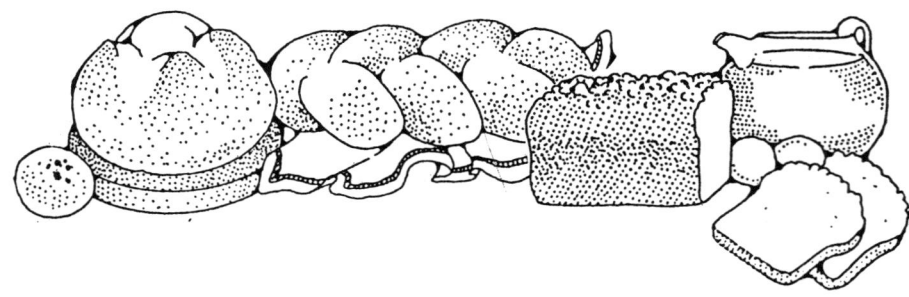

6 | Vitamins

The importance of vitamins

Vitamins are organic substances that our bodies require in small quantities to ensure our health and normal body function.

Our bodies cannot alone produce most vitamins; therefore, we must obtain them from various types of food. Upon entering the body, the vitamins divide into small units and are dispersed.

When a person's diet lacks vitamins, or when one is unable to properly absorb vitamins (due to prolonged diarrhea or similar problems), there awakens the danger of specific vitamin deficiencies in the body. For example, a person who, for whatever reason, does not eat fruits or vegetables for several months is likely to develop a vitamin deficiency, with all the dependent secondary effects.

An infant who is sensitive to milk and milk products, or to gluten (one of the proteins in wheat), and continues to be fed these foods, is likely to suffer from prolonged diarrhea, which will cause severe vitamin deficiencies.

In general, the vitamins are divided into two groups: fat-soluble vitamins, including vitamins A, D, E, and K; and water-soluble vitamins: vitamin C and the B-group vitamins (thiamin, riboflavin, niacin, vitamin B_6, folacin, and vitamin B_{12}, as well as pantothenic acid and biotin).

To remain healthy, a person needs to vary his daily nutritional menu in such a way that he will obtain all the vitamins that he requires. It is therefore recommended to eat from all types of food — in the appropriate amounts.

Does an overdose of Vitamin C affect our bodies?

All nutritionists agree that it is worthwhile for everyone to receive a regular, daily amount of vitamin C — about 60 mg. per day. Any amount in excess of this quantity that one consumes is excreted from his body.

There is a type of cold virus that vitamin C protects us from; nevertheless, presently there is no conclusive evidence that overload of this vitamin has a greater immunizing effect. A dose of 100 to 200 mg. of vitamin C does not pose any risk and may be helpful.

On the other hand, an exaggerated dose of vitamin C, such as 2 to 5 g. per day (1 g. = 1,000 mg.), carries the risk that the body may become dependent on this quantity, and that in the future, in the event of slight decreases in this daily megadose, one may exhibit the dangerous state of vitamin C deficiency. Furthermore, an excessively large quantity of vitamin C taken over a prolonged period of time is likely to cause an elevation of blood cholesterol.

In summation, everyone requires vitamin C, and one should receive this vitamin daily, if possible, but in measured and not exaggerated amounts! Taking significantly more vitamin C when one has a cold is not dangerous, and it may shorten the duration of the illness.

Vitamin C in Foods

Food	Quantity	Vitamin C (milligrams)
CITRUS FRUITS		
Grapefruit, pink	1/2 medium	47
Grapefruit, white	1/2 medium	39
Lemon	1 medium	31
Lime	1 medium	20
Orange	1 medium	80
Tangerine	1 medium	26
JUICES		
Grapefruit juice	8 fl. oz.	94
Lemonade	8 fl. oz.	112
Limeade	8 fl. oz.	72
Orange juice	8 fl. oz.	124
Tomato juice	8 fl. oz.	102
OTHER FRUITS		
Blackberries	1/2 cup	15
Cantaloupe	1 cup	68
Currants, black	1/2 cup	101
Guava	1 medium	165
Honeydew melon	1/4 small	23
Kiwifruit	1 medium	75
Mango	1 medium	57
Papaya	1 medium	188
Pineapple pieces	1 cup	24
Raspberries	1 cup	31
Strawberries	1 cup	85
Watermelon	1 cup	15

VEGETABLES

Asparagus, cooked	2/3 cup	26
Broccoli, cooked	1 large stalk	90
Brussels sprouts, cooked	6-8 medium	87
Cabbage, green, shredded	1 cup	47
Cabbage, red, shredded	1 cup	61
Cauliflower, cooked	7/8 cup	55
Kale	3 oz.	107
Kohlrabi, cooked	2/3 cup	43
Parsley	3 oz.	147
Peas, cooked	2/3 cup	20
Pepper, green	1 large	128
Potato, baked	1 medium	20
Potato, boiled	1 medium	16
Radish, red	10 small	26
Sauerkraut	2/3 cup	16
Scallions	5 medium	25
Sweet potato, baked	1 small	22
Tomato	1 medium	34

What is Vitamin E?

Vitamin E is one of the fat-soluble vitamins. It is not entirely known exactly what effect this vitamin has on man. Popular opinion is that vitamin E has a positive benefit in avoiding miscarriages, in easing muscle pain, in decreasing acne, and with regard to other ailments. There is as yet no scientific proof that adding vitamin E will actually help in these areas. In animal experiments, vitamin E has had a specific effect, though no such effect has been proven in humans. There are no known illnesses resulting from vitamin E deficiency. One receives this vitamin in his usual foods.

Which fruits are most nutritious?

Fruits are produced from the flower and are the ripened ovary (seeds) of a plant, with surrounding tissues. The main component of fruits is water, which constitutes 75 to 90% of the fruit. After water, carbohydrates are the main components of fruits, in the form of sugars, starches, cellulose, and pectin; and they are the source of energy and structure.

Most fruits have only a trace of fat and a small amount of protein. On the other hand, fruits are a valuable source of vitamins and minerals as well as fiber. Some are important sources of ascorbic acid (vitamin C), such as citrus fruits (including oranges, grapefruits, and lemons), certain melons, guava, and strawberries.

Other fruits, especially those with a yellow color (including apricots, cantaloupe, and peaches), are sources of vitamin A (carotene). B-vitamins occur in relatively low concentrations in fruits, as do calcium, phosphorus, and iron. Exceptions to this rule include several iron-containing fruits, such as strawberries, dried apricots, prunes, dates, and figs, and certain fruits that are fair sources of calcium, such as oranges, grapefruits, and figs.

Fruits are eaten in many forms: fresh, cooked, canned, frozen, dried, pureed, baked, or juiced. Most fresh fruits are consumed raw, and this is recommended whenever possible, for fruits are generally nutritionally at their best in the raw state.

Processing usually reduces the vitamin content of fruit, which may be significant in relation to vitamin C. Long-term storage of fruits may decrease vitamin values as much as 50%. Fruits should be eaten when ripe and not before in order to assure maximum vitamin C content and digestibility.

Drying of fruits reduces their water content to less than 30% and usually eliminates vitamin C. This is only relevant, however, with regard to those fruits that contain significant amounts of vitamin C. Cooking, baking, and canning lower or eliminate vitamin C from food, depending upon the degree of heat and the length of processing time.

Crushing and squeezing of fruits somewhat lower their vitamin C content. However, frozen orange juice may have a high vitamin C content, despite having been squeezed out, if the fruit was frozen as soon as it was picked and thus did not require long-term storage, which would have had a greater vitamin-lowering effect.

Nutritional Values of Some Fruits

Fruit	Quantity (3 oz.)	Energy (cal.)	Protein (g.)	Carbohydrate (g.)	Fat (g.)	Iron (mg.)	Vit. C (mg.)
Grapes	25	57	0.6	13.2	0.2	0.4	3
Raisins	2/3 cup	296	2.5	70.4	0.5	2.5	0
Fresh figs	2	74	1.3	16	0.4	2.9	2
Dried figs	5	261	4	58.6	1.2	3.8	0
Persimmon	1	77	0.7	19.7	0.4	0.3	11
Pomegranate	2/3	62	0.4	14.7	0.2	0.4	5
Fresh dates	11	134	0.9	32	0.3	1	9
Dried dates	12	234	1.8	55.6	0.5	1.7	0
Olives	20	113	1.1	2.3	11.1	1	0
Plums	3	46	0.6	10.4	0.2	0.4	5
Prunes	12	175	1.7	41	0.3	2.4	0
Fresh apricots	3	47	0.7	10.6	0.2	0.7	10
Dried apricots	14 1/2	300	4.5	68	1.1	4.5	0

Vitamins: Summary

WATER-SOLUBLE VITAMINS

ASCORBIC ACID (vitamin C)
> Function: Maintains normal intercellular material of cartilage, dentin, and bone; associated with oxidation-reduction systems in tissues; metabolizes some amino acids (tyrosine, phenylalanine); promotes the healing of wounds and fractures; reduces liability to infection; enhances iron absorption.
> Main sources: citrus fruits, melons, tomatoes, strawberries, raw cabbage, potatoes, green peppers, red peppers, kiwifruit.

THIAMIN (vitamin B_1)
> Function: Part of cocarboxylase, aiding in the removal of carbon dioxide from alphaketo acids during carbohydrate oxidation; essential for growth, normal appetite, digestion, and healthy nerves.
> Main sources: whole-grain or enriched cereals and breads, potatoes, soybeans, peanuts, organ meats.

RIBOFLAVIN (vitamin B_2)
> Function: Enzymatic role in tissue reproduction, and transportation of hydrogen ions.
> Main sources: milk, organ meats, green leafy vegetables, enriched breads and cereals, eggs.

NIACIN (nicotinic acid)
> Function: Enzymatic role of aiding in the transfer of hydrogen, and in carbohydrate and amino acid metabolism.
> Main sources: meat, poultry, fish, many grains, eggs, milk, legumes, enriched grains, peanuts.

VITAMIN B_6 (pyridoxine, pyridoxal, and pyridoxamine)
> Function: Coenzyme aiding in the synthesis and breakdown of amino acids and in the synthesis of unsaturated fatty acids from essential fatty acids; essential for the conversion of tryptophan to niacin.
> Main sources: cereal bran and germ, milk, egg yolk, oatmeal, legumes.

VITAMIN B$_{12}$ (cyanocobalamin)
   Function: Role in the metabolism of single-carbon fragments; needed for the biosynthesis of nucleic acids and nucleoproteins (as in normal red blood cell formation); role in nervous tissue metabolism; probably essential for fat metabolism.
   Main sources: milk and milk products, eggs, meat.

PANTOTHENIC ACID
   Function: Part of coenzyme A; essential in intermediary metabolism of carbohydrate, protein, and fat.
   Main sources: all plant and animal foods.

FOLACIN (folic acid)
   Function: Role in the biosynthesis of nucleic acids, the maturation of red blood cells, and probably essential for normal fat metabolism; functions as a coenzyme, tetrahydro-folic acid.
   Main sources: green leafy vegetables, organ meats, wheat, eggs, fish, dry beans, lentils, asparagus, broccoli.

BIOTIN
   Function: Role in the synthesis and breakdown of fatty acids and amino acids through aiding the addition and removal of carbon dioxide to or from active compounds, and the removal of ammonia from amino acids.
   Main sources: synthesized in the intestinal tract; most vegetables, milk, meat, egg yolk, bananas, tomatoes, grapefruit.

FAT-SOLUBLE VITAMINS

VITAMIN A (retinol, pro-vitamin A, alpha-, beta-, gamma-carotene)
   Function: Essential for normal growth and maintenance of epithelial tissue, normal bone development, tooth formation, health of the eyes and night vision; toxic in large amounts.
   Main sources: yellow, orange and dark green leafy vegetables and fruits, liver, milk fat, fortified margarine, egg yolk.

VITAMIN D (calciferol)
>Function: Essential for normal growth, bone and tooth formation; influences the absorption and utilization of phosphorus and calcium.
>Main sources: vitamin D milk, irradiated foods.

VITAMIN E (tocopherol)
>Function: May help prevent oxidation of unsaturated fatty acids and vitamin A in the intestinal tract and body tissues; protects red blood cells from hemolysis.
>Main sources: wheat germ, vegetable oils, green leafy vegetables, milk fat, egg yolk, nuts.

VITAMIN K (menadione)
>Function: Aids in the production of prothrombin for normal blood clotting.
>Main sources: vegetable oils, green leafy vegetables, tomatoes, cauliflower, wheat bran, liver.

*Better is a dinner of herbs where love is
than a fatted ox and hatred with it.*

MISHLEI 15:17

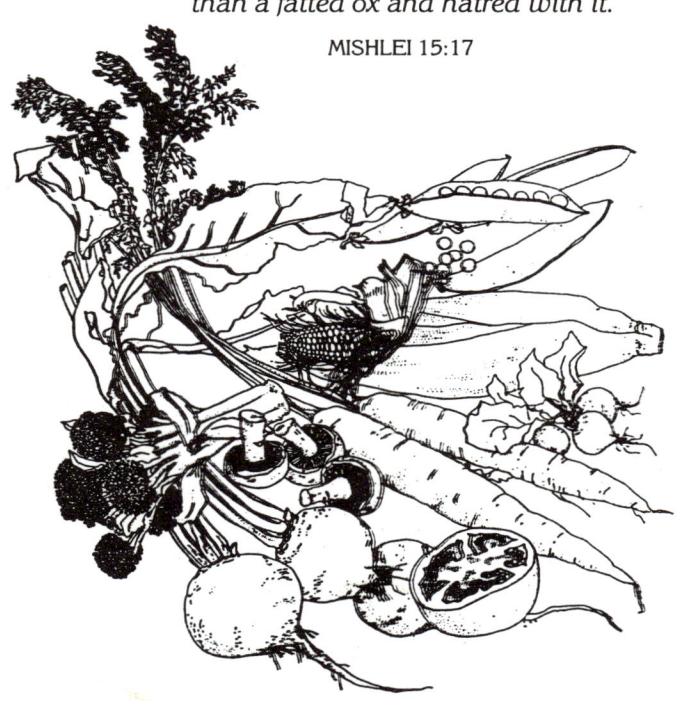

7 | Minerals

What is the importance of calcium in our diet?

Calcium is an inorganic or non-carbon-containing mineral and nutrient. It is essential to the body as a fundamental building element and component of many essential processes. Approximately 2% of the adult human body is calcium. Ninety-nine percent of the calcium in the body is used in building bones and teeth in the young and in maintenance in the adult. Small amounts of calcium are also required for normal nerve and muscle function, and for normal blood clotting. Lack of an adequate calcium intake over extended periods of time may result in the disease known as osteoporosis. This appears as a general weakening of the skeletal structure, which is complicated by brittleness of the bones and frequent fractures.

What are the main dietary sources of calcium?

Milk is known for its supreme importance in our daily nourishment. From the first day in the life of the infant, milk is the main source of nutrition. It contains all the essential amino acids as well as calcium and phosphorus. Milk contains 87% water and 5% carbohydrate in the form of lactose (milk-sugar). It contains from 1-3.8% fat. It is a significant source of vitamin B_2, vitamin A, and niacin, and it provides a small amount of vitamin B_1.

Milk and milk products (yogurt and cheese) are the most important sources of calcium in readily available form. Green leafy vegetables which contain significant amounts of calcium also contain oxalic acid, which forms insoluble calcium oxalate, rendering the calcium unavailable. Sardines and other small fish whose bones are eaten are important sources of calcium. Soybeans and molasses are minor sources of calcium.

Calcium in Foods

Food	Quantity	Calcium (milligrams)
Almonds	12-15 nuts	38
Brazil nuts	2 medium	28
Broccoli, cooked	1 large stalk	88
Cottage cheese	1 cup	126
Figs, dried	1	26.9
Goat's milk	1 cup	326
Kale, cooked	3/4 cup	134
Milk	1 cup	290
Molasses	1 tbsp.	140
Orange	1 medium	56
Salmon, pink	3 oz.	176
Sardines	8 medium	354
Sesame seeds, hulled	2 tbsp.	25
Sesame seeds, whole	2 tbsp.	290
Sour cream	1 tbsp.	14
Soybean nuts	1 oz.	68
Soybeans, cooked	1 cup	130
Tofu (soybean curd)	3 oz.	110
White cheese	3 oz.	104
Yellow cheese	3 oz.	666
Yogurt	1 cup	270

Sesame seed butter, or techina made from whole ground seeds, is a rich source of calcium, two tablespoons yielding the same amount of calcium as is in a glass of milk.

For optimal absorption, calcium should be taken together with adequate sources of phosphorus, lactose (milk-sugar), and vitamin D (which is naturally provided in milk and in milk products).

How much calcium does one need?

The U.S. Recommended Dietary Allowances for adults is 800 mg. of calcium per day. The calcium allowances during pregnancy and lactation are increased to 1,200 mg. per day to cover fetal needs and the calcium required to produce human milk. Lack of dietary calcium is now considered the major cause of osteoporosis in women. This is due to increased calcium needs during pregnancies and lactation with inadequate dietary calcium intakes over extended periods of time. Research has now shown that consistent adequate calcium intakes can prevent osteoporosis, increasing bone strength and decreasing incidents of bone fractures in later life.

How can one deal with a milk allergy?

For children who suffer from true milk allergy, one can obtain, today, milk-free formula, ensuring optimal nutrition in the child's first formative years. However, what is commonly called a "milk allergy" is usually due to faulty digestion and is not a true allergic response to a foreign protein entering the body.

A lack of the enzyme lactase is the reason many persons, especially adults, are unable to properly digest milk or milk products. This enzyme is necessary in order to break down the milk-sugar (or lactose) contained in milk for absorption into the body. When someone with a lactase deficiency consumes large amounts of a lactose-containing food at one time, the milk-sugar passes undigested through the stomach and into the intestines, where it absorbs a lot of water and becomes food for intestinal bacteria that form gases and acids. This results in such symptoms as abdominal bloating, gas, cramps, and diarrhea.

There is much individual variety in the degree of lactose intolerance, and people may vary greatly in the amounts of milk or milk products that they may safely consume.

However, even in the lactose-intolerant the problem can usually be controlled without their giving up the consumption of dairy products, which, we have seen, are the most important source of calcium, necessary for strong bones and teeth. (Temporary lactose-intolerance may result from certain conditions or illnesses.) One may be able to eat lactose-containing products as long as not too much lactose is eaten at once. For example, small amounts of milk several times a day, instead of one large glass at one time, may be tolerated. Dairy products such as yogurt, sour cream, and cheese may be tolerated, as the lactose in these foods has been partly digested. Hard cheeses contain very little lactose. Milk-containing foods consumed hot are often better tolerated than cold ones.

Except for those who are highly sensitive, people with lactose-intolerance can consume milk that has been treated with the lactase enzyme. This may be achieved by putting 4 to 8 drops of "Lactaid" (lactase enzyme, available at most pharmacies) in a quart of milk, mixing well, and leaving it refrigerated for twenty-four hours. It can then be used just like regular milk, but it has a slightly sweeter taste. Even better, the new "Lactaid" pill, which can be taken together with milk without any preparation, is now available.

Iron — What is it good for?

Vitamins have a great effect on the hemoglobin level (red blood cells), but iron — which is not a vitamin but a mineral — has the decisive effect. Iron is essentially part of the hemoglobin molecule, and the role of the vitamins is to attach the iron to this molecule. If the quantity of nutritional iron in the expectant woman is low for too long a period of time, this will cause her to have a low hemoglobin, with a resultant lowering of her baby's hemoglobin count.

The main food sources of iron include red meat, chicken, eggs, most green vegetables, raisins, potatoes, whole-grain cereals, dried fruits, peas and beans. All of these — or at least most — should be included in the regular daily nutritional plan of all persons and especially of pregnant women.

In order to insert the mineral iron into the hemoglobin molecule, the body must receive sufficient quantities of vitamins C, E, and B_{12}, which are responsible for the absorption of iron into the hemoglobin.

Iron in Foods

Food	Quantity	Iron (milligrams)
Almonds	12-15	0.7
Apricots, dried	5 halves	1.5
Beans, cooked	1/2 cup	2.1
Beef, cooked	3 oz.	2.7
Beet greens, cooked	1/2 cup	2.4
Bran flakes	1/2 cup	0.8
Brazil nuts	2 medium	0.5
Bread, whole wheat	1 slice	0.6
Cashews	6-8	0.8
Chocolate, bitter	1 square	1.3
Chocolate, sweet	1 square	0.8
Cocoa	1 tbsp.	0.8
Coconut, dried	2 tbsp.	0.5
Coconut, fresh	1/2 oz.	0.3
Cornmeal, degermed, enriched, cooked	1/2 cup	0.4
Currants, dried	2 tbsp.	0.8
Dates	3-4	0.6
Egg, whole	1	1.4

Egg, yolk	1	1.4
Figs, dried	2 small	0.9
Flour, enriched	2 tbsp.	0.4
Flour, whole wheat	2 tbsp.	0.5
Hazelnuts	10-12	0.6
Kale	3/4 cup	1.7
Lamb, leg	3 oz.	2.9
Lentils, cooked	1/2 cup	2.2
Liver, beef	3 oz.	7.1
Molasses, blackstrap	1 tbsp.	3.2
Molasses, light	1 tbsp.	0.9
Oatmeal, cooked	1/2 cup	0.7
Parsley	10 sprigs	0.4
Peas, cooked	1/2 cup	1.4
Pecans	12 halves	0.4
Popcorn, popped	1 cup	0.4
Prunes	4	1.2
Raisins	5 tbsp.	1.7
Rice, brown, cooked	1/2 cup	0.3
Rye, whole-meal	1 tbsp.	0.6
Sardines	3 oz.	2.4
Soybeans, cooked	1/2 cup	4.4
Spinach, cooked	1/2 cup	1.5
Sugar, brown	1 tbsp.	0.4
Tongue, beef	3 oz.	2.6
Turkey	3 oz.	3.5
Turnip greens	1/2 cup	1.8
Walnuts	8	0.3
Wheat flakes	1/2 cup	0.5
Yeast, compressed	1 oz.	1.5
Yeast, dried	2 tbsp.	2.7

Minerals: Summary

MACROMINERALS

CALCIUM
    Function: Ionic calcium in body fluids is essential for ion transport across cell membranes.
    Main sources: milk and milk products, greens, broccoli, sardines.

IRON
    Function: Component of hemoglobin and myoglobin, and it is important in oxygen transfer, in serum transfer and certain enzymes.
    Main sources: meat, liver, chicken, egg yolk, legumes, whole or enriched grains, dark green vegetables, dark molasses, dried fruits, potatoes, peas, beans.

POTASSIUM
    Function: A major mineral component of intracellular fluid; functions in regulating pH (acidity) and osmolarity (concentration), and cell membrane transfer; an ion needed for carbohydrate and protein metabolism.
    Main sources: fruits, milk, meat, cereals, vegetables, legumes.

MAGNESIUM
    Function: Activator of many enzymes affecting almost all metabolic processes.
    Main sources: whole-grain cereals, nuts, meat, milk, legumes, green vegetables.

Other macrominerals include phosphorus, sodium, chlorine, and sulfur.

MICROMINERALS

ZINC
    Function: Constituent of essential enzymes and insulin; possible importance in nucleic acid metabolism; role in wound healing and in taste acuity.
    Main sources: milk, wheat bran, liver, herring.

CHROMIUM
> Function: Associated with glucose metabolism.
> Main sources: corn oil, whole-grain cereals, meat, drinking water (variable).

IODINE
> Function: Component of thyroxine and related compounds synthesized by the thyroid gland, functioning in control of cellular energy reactions.
> Main sources: iodized table salt, seafood, water and vegetables in iodine-rich regions.

Other microminerals include copper, manganese, fluorine, molybdenum, cobalt, selenium, nickel, tin, vanadium, and silicon.

*As cold water to a thirsty soul,
so is good news from a far country.*

MISHLEI 25:25

8 | Fluid

How much fluid does one need?

Appetite and thirst, in the body of a healthy person, function in a natural and independent way. Thirst initiates a reflex that sends us to the nearest faucet or to our drinking cup — without our investing any special thought.

The thirst center is located in the brain, in the hypothalamus, and in the healthy person there exists a natural perception of thirst, so to speak. An ill person, whose sense of thirst is defective, needs first and foremost a balancing of fluid in his body, since this is at times his medicine of life.

The water that our body needs has its origin in what we drink as well as in the liquids found in most types of food. A normal person receives 25 fl. oz. of liquid through the food he eats, and 55 fl. oz. through drinking, while digestion of food and metabolism contribute an additional 12 fl. oz. — a total of 92 fl. oz. of liquid per day. Each person should drink 6 to 8 cups (48-64 fl. oz.) of liquid a day. In the summer months, this amount should be increased.

Just as it enters the body, this quantity of daily fluid also leaves it. Through the pores of the skin (via sweating) one loses 17 fl. oz. of liquid (on a normal day), through the respiratory tract one loses 13 fl. oz., from the kidneys (as urine) 57 fl. oz., and through the intestines (as stool) 5 fl. oz. — a total of 92 fl. oz.

At times, during large fluid loss — due to sweating, vomiting, diarrhea or other conditions — it is necessary to add water to the body, above the previously mentioned amounts. It is very important to preserve the water balance of the body. In a hot environment, or during the summer, when there is intense sweating, one should drink more. During the winter one sweats less and therefore needs to drink less.

Is herbal tea really healthier than regular tea?

Herbal teas can be recommended for three reasons:

1. Herbal teas generally do not contain nerve-stimulating caffeine, which is contained in regular tea. The amount of caffeine consumed in the latter would depend on the strength of the tea, a strong tea having a caffeine content equivalent to that of coffee.

2. Regular tea can have a constipating effect (depending on the frequency of consumption and the concentration of the tea, as well as the sensitivity of the drinker) due to a substance in it known as tannin.

3. Recent research with laboratory animals shows increased incidence of cancer associated with high intakes of regular teas. (Further investigation is, of course, required here.) Added dyes in teas may also produce an unhealthy effect which must be clarified.

On the other hand, the healthy effects of herbal teas should not be underestimated. Herbal teas may be helpful in relieving indigestion, gas, and stomach pain.

Caffeine in Foods

Food	Quantity	Caffeine (*milligrams*)
COFFEE		
Drip, automatic	5 fl. oz.	137
Drip, nonautomatic	5 fl. oz.	124
Instant	5 fl. oz.	60
Instant, decaffeinated	5 fl. oz.	3
Percolated, automatic	5 fl. oz.	117
Percolated, nonautomatic	5 fl. oz.	108
TEA		
American black, 1 min. brew	5 fl. oz.	28
American black, 3 min. brew	5 fl. oz.	42
American black, 5 min. brew	5 fl. oz.	46
Decaffeinated, 5 min. brew	6 fl. oz.	1
Green, 1 min. brew	5 fl. oz.	14
Green, 3 min. brew	5 fl. oz.	27
Green, 5 min. brew	5 fl. oz.	31
Instant	5 fl. oz.	28
SOFT DRINKS		
Coca-Cola	12 fl. oz.	45
Cola, decaffeinated	12 fl. oz.	trace
Diet Coke	12 fl. oz.	45
Pepsi Cola	12 fl. oz.	38
Pepsi, diet	12 fl. oz.	36
CHOCOLATE AND FOODS CONTAINING CHOCOLATE		
Baking chocolate	1 oz.	35
Chocolate brownie	1 1/4 oz.	8

Chocolate cake	1/16 of a 9 in. cake	14
Chocolate covered candy	1 oz.	3
Chocolate ice cream	2/3 cup	5
Chocolate milk	8 fl. oz.	5
Chocolate pudding, instant	1/2 cup	6
Chocolate syrup	2 tbsp.	4
Cocoa, dry powder	1 tbsp.	11
Milk chocolate	1 oz.	6
Milk chocolate chips	1/4 cup	8
Semi-sweet chocolate	1 oz.	12
Sweet chocolate, dark	1 oz.	20

PART II:
Eating Well

APPLIED PRINCIPLES

There is no festivity without eating and drinking.

Mo'ed Katan 9a

Rabbi Yochanan and Rabbi Elazar said, "As long as the Temple stood, the sacrificial altar atoned for Israel; now a man's table atones for him."

Berachos 55a

1 | General guidelines

The seven dietary guidelines

The 1988 report of the United States Surgeon General on nutrition and health is the most comprehensive governmental review of the connection between diet and health, drawing on more than 2,000 studies. In powerful terms, the report states that diet helped account for more than two-thirds of the 2.1 million deaths in 1987 in the United States. Poor nutritional habits were strongly implicated in five of the country's top ten killers, including coronary heart disease, stroke, atherosclerosis, diabetes, and some cancers; and excessive alcohol use was linked to another three causes. The report stresses that, aside from drinking alcohol and smoking, diet is the "one personal choice" that, more than any other, influences long-term health prospects.

With this in mind and considering the present knowledge available in the field of nutrition, the United States Department of Agriculture published the following seven recommendations, in order to promote optimal health in the general population:

1. Eat a variety of foods.

2. Maintain a desirable weight.

3. Avoid too much fat, saturated fat, and cholesterol.

4. Choose a diet with plenty of vegetables, fruits, and grain products.

5. Avoid too much sugar.

6. Avoid too much salt (sodium).

7. If you drink alcoholic beverages, do so in moderation.

Let us discuss these guidelines in more detail:

1. Eat a variety of foods every day.

To ensure an adequate intake of all essential nutrients, it is important to eat a variety of foods each day. It is therefore advisable to eat daily portions of fruits (fresh or dried) and vegetables, breads and cereals (emphasizing whole-grain products), milk and milk products (limited as much as possible in fat content), meat, chicken, and fish (low-fat preferred), eggs (a maximum of three per week is presently recommended), seeds, beans, and peas.

2. Maintain a desirable weight.

To lose weight, eat less fat and fatty foods. Limit, as well, the intake of foods high in added sugar or sweets. Eat more vegetables, fruits, and whole grains. For more precise instruction to ensure a nutritionally adequate diet, arrange for consultation with a qualified, professional nutritionist or dietitian. An increase in daily physical activity is desirable, as well as an overall improvement of eating habits, to achieve successful permanent weight reduction.

3. Avoid too much fat, saturated fat, and cholesterol.

Use milk products with the lowest amount of fat available, such as 1% milk and low-fat cheese. Choose lean meat, chicken, and fish, and limit the use of liver and other organ meats. Increase the use of beans and peas in place of meats as protein sources. It is presently recommended to limit the intake of egg yolks to three per week. Limit the intake of fats and fatty foods high in saturated fat, such as butter, cream, shortenings, and foods containing palm and coconut oils. Fat intake should be limited to 30% of the total calories. Of this

30%, one-third or less should be from sources of saturated fat, one-third from monounsaturated fats and oils, and one-third from polyunsaturated oils. Persons with a high cholesterol level (above 240) should arrange for consultation with a qualified, professional nutritionist or dietitian for dietary instruction.

4. Choose a diet with plenty of vegetables, fruits, and grain products.

Substitute starchy foods (complex carbohydrates) for those having large amounts of fats and sugars. Choose whole-grain breads and cereals, fruits, vegetables, and beans and peas as sources of increased fiber.

5. Avoid too much sugar.

Use less of all foods containing large amounts of sugars. Examples of such foods include soft drinks, candies, cakes, and cookies.

6. Avoid too much salt (sodium).

Cook without salt or with only small amounts of added salt. In place of salt, flavor foods with herbs, spices, or lemon juice. Add little or no salt to food at the table. Also, limit your intake of salty foods such as pretzels, salted nuts and seeds, salt-containing condiments (such as garlic salt), and pickled foods.

7. Drink alcoholic beverages only in moderation, if at all.

Limited amounts of alcohol consumption appear to cause no harm in normal, healthy, nonpregnant adults.

These guidelines refer to optimal dietary patterns rather than to levels of specific nutrients. Persons with problems in particular areas mentioned are urged to arrange for professional nutrition consultation at the earliest opportunity.

JEWISH GUIDE TO NATURAL NUTRITION

Food Guide Pyramid
A Guide to Daily Food Choices

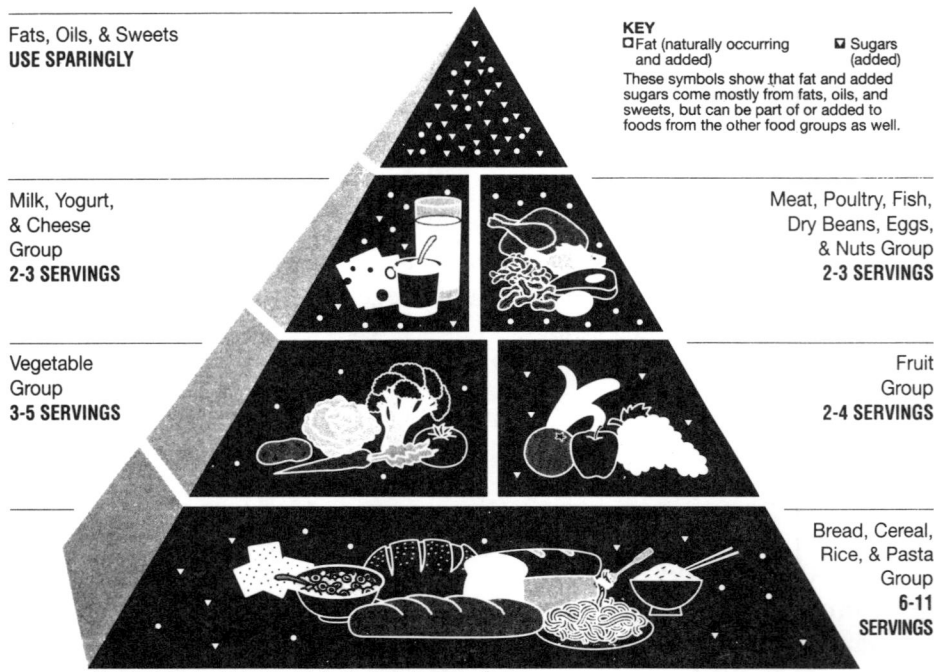

SOURCE: U.S. Department of Agriculture/U.S. Department of Health and Human Services

WHAT COUNTS AS A SERVING?

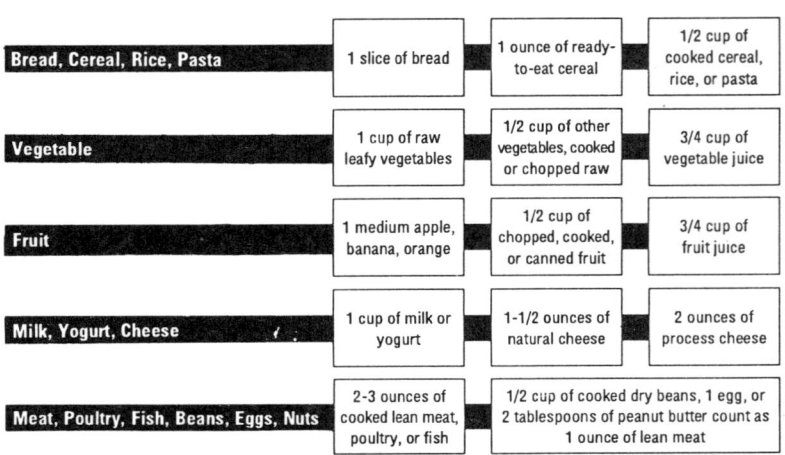

The food guide pyramid

The "Food Guide Pyramid" illustrates the recent change in emphasis regarding the various food groups. Foods recommended as the basis of the daily diet are located at the base of the pyramid. As one ascends to the top of the pyramid, one encounters the foods which should be eaten in lesser amounts. In summary, the major components of the daily diet should be from the bread and cereals group, followed by the vegetables and fruits. Protein foods, such as milk products, meat, poultry, fish, eggs, and legumes (peas, beans), are less emphasized. Fats, oils, and sweets are the least promoted and should be eaten only in small amounts. This is essentially the basic low-fat (low-cholesterol), high-fiber eating plan recommended previously in the seven dietary guidelines.

This new way of eating will substantially reduce your risk of developing many negative health conditions and diseases, including obesity, high blood pressure, stroke, osteoporosis, diabetes, gallstones, and cancers of the colon, breast, and prostate. In addition, you will have more energy, think more clearly, improve your physical performance — in short, look better, feel better, and enjoy your life more!

Recommendations

BREADS, CEREALS, RICE AND PASTA
    6-11 daily servings. A serving could be 1 slice of bread, 1/2 a bun or bagel, 1 ounce of dry cereal or 1/2 cup of cooked cereal, rice or pasta.

VEGETABLES
    3-5 daily servings. A serving could be 1 cup of raw, leafy greens or 1/2 cup of any other vegetable.

FRUITS
    2-4 daily servings. A serving could be 1 medium apple, banana or orange; 1/2 cup of fresh, cooked or canned fruit; or 3/4 cup of fruit juice.

MILK, YOGURT AND CHEESE
   2-3 daily servings. A serving could be 1 cup of milk, 8 oz. of yogurt, 1 1/2 oz. of natural cheese or 2 oz. of processed cheese.

MEAT, POULTRY, FISH, DRY BEANS & PEAS, EGGS, NUTS & SEEDS
   2-3 daily servings. That totals 5-7 oz. of cooked lean meat, poultry or fish a day. Could be 1/2 cup of cooked beans, 1 egg or 2 tbsp. of peanut butter as 1 oz. of meat.

2 | Natural cooking

Good nutrition can be ensured by eating a varied diet of fresh, wholesome foods. These foods should be, as much as possible, unrefined and high in complex carbohydrates and fiber, adequate but not excessive in protein, and low in fat, cholesterol, and salt.

Eating for health is important and can be an exciting discovery experience. Grains, legumes, and vegetables are the foundations of the diet. You will find new foods in supermarkets, local food stores, and natural food shops. You will discover a new eating experience with vibrant food colors, rich flavors, a variety of textures and, in general, a larger variety of foods. You will relearn the childhood joy of eating crunchy vegetables and sweet, juicy fruits, and will enjoy the natural tastes of herbs and spices.

These changes, however, cannot and should not be made overnight. Gradually improving your diet is the best way to ensure good health and long-term change. Begin by reducing high-fat foods, especially fatty meats, fried foods, eggs, and milk products high in fat. Then take one step at a time, progressing to a diet based on grains and legumes, with generous amounts of vegetables and fruits, low-fat milk products, and, if you wish, low-fat fish and poultry.

Begin altering your favorite recipes, cooking those you already enjoy in a healthier way. Try to make the same recipe but omit the meat or the oil. Replace the meat with cooked whole grains, beans, or finely chopped vegetables. You will often be able to leave out or reduce the amount of oil without significantly altering the final product. Instead of sautéing in oil or margarine, cook vegetables in a small amount of water or steam them. Add some lemon juice, vegetable stock, or apple cider vinegar to spark up the taste. For salad dressings, in place of oil or to reduce the amount of oil, use vinegars, lemon juice, or tomato or orange juice. You can try substituting two egg whites for each egg yolk when you bake. You can use fruits, fruit juice, or fruit juice concentrates as your sweenening agents.

Relaxed eating

Before we begin discussing the details of how to apply the "Eating Well" principles, let us take a break and consider how we should approach our meals and snacks. A very important part of eating well is not just what we eat but also *how* we eat!

It is best to take meals and snacks at the same time every day, in a relaxed, positive setting. Avoid skipping meals, especially breakfast, as doing so will weaken your body. Going for long periods of time without adequate nutrition leads to fatigue, low blood sugar, loss of concentration, headaches, and increased stress.

Stress, from whatever source, is very damaging to the digestion. The stomach and neck tense up after hearing bad news or during aggravating discussions full of complaints and negativity. Can you feel yourself tensing as you picture this?

Now relax, and learn to relax before, during, and after eating. It is a good idea to relax more during your entire day, to ensure your continued good health.

Sit with a good posture. Slow down. Do not gobble up your food as if you have not eaten for days. Try to have positive conversations and happy thoughts during your meals. Make meal times happy times.

Relaxing before eating will improve your digestion, allowing your digestive glands (the parotids and the sublinguals) to produce the necessary digestive enzymes. To help yourself relax you may wish to try a progressive relaxation technique or some deep breathing. Imagine your stomach muscles relaxing, and they will relax. Release all tension from your body, and clear your mind. Repeat a positive statement over and over to yourself, either mentally or aloud. Tell yourself that you are relaxed and ready to begin eating in a healthy way. A prayer said before eating will make you fully aware of Who is in ultimate control, and Who has graciously provided the food you are about to enjoy.

Eat slowly, and chew your food thoroughly. Digestion begins in the mouth, with each well-chewed bite. Limit fluids during meals to one small glass, and drink ample fluids between meals (6 to 8 glasses per day). In this way you will not dilute the essential digestive juices of the mouth and stomach. Slowing down the pace of eating will also help you avoid overeating.

Yaakov Levinson's Guide to Good Eating

The "Guide to Good Eating" consists basically of a low-fat (low-cholesterol), high-fiber eating plan, as previously discussed. The main foods are outlined as follows:

WHOLE GRAINS — breads and cereals

LEGUMES — peas and beans

ALL VEGETABLES
  including potatoes and sweet potatoes

ALL FRUITS — including a vitamin C source daily

ANIMAL PRODUCTS — low-fat, limited amounts;
  low-fat milk, yogurt, cheeses, egg whites (yolks limited), fish, chicken, turkey, lean meat (no skin)

OILS — cold-pressed, limited amounts;
  preferably: olive or canola
  alternatives: safflower, corn, soy, sunflower, sesame;
  nuts and seeds, limited amounts

BEVERAGES
  water, fresh fruit juices, fruit juice concentrates, herbal teas, grain coffees, mineral waters, vegetable juices

Avoid or limit refined flours and cereals, white sugar, fried foods, caffeine-containing beverages (such as coffee, tea, and cola), alcoholic beverages, and salt. To bring out the natural taste in foods, use herbs and spices, garlic, lemon, vinegars, fruit concentrates, and honeys. Choose apples, celery, carrot sticks, raisins, vegetable soup, and oranges as healthy snacks.

WHOLE GRAINS
(breads and cereals)

BARLEY

BROWN RICE, RICE CREAM, RICE FLOUR

BUCKWHEAT (Kasha), BUCKWHEAT FLOUR

BULGUR

CORN, CORNMEAL, CORN FLOUR

MILLET

OATS (rolled, cut), OAT BRAN

RYE, RYE FLOUR

TEFF

WHEAT BERRIES, WHOLE-WHEAT FLOUR, WHEAT GERM, WHEAT BRAN

QUALITIES AND PREPARATION OF WHOLE GRAINS

Grains are the seeds of grasses. Each grain contains a seed (germ), food for the seed (endosperm), and a covering to protect the seed and the food source (hull and bran). Milling and refining remove the germ and bran layers to process the grains into flours. Whole grains, on the other hand, contain all three components: germ, endosperm, and bran. Whole grains therefore contain nutrients — such as more protein, B-vitamins, iron, essential fats, and fiber — that are otherwise removed during the refining process. Use whole-grain breads and cereals, muffins, cakes, crackers, noodles and pastas.

BARLEY

Barley has a chewy texture and nutty taste. It looks like rice and expands when cooked. It is useful as a thickener and in soups. To prepare, add 3 parts water to 1 part grain. Bring it to a boil, cover and simmer for 1 hour.

BROWN RICE

The whole, unpolished rice grain has a nutty, wholesome flavor. Brown rice comes in long- and short-grain varieties. It provides high-quality protein when eaten together with beans. Brown rice is an excellent source of fiber, B-vitamins, and complex carbohydrate. To prepare, add 2 parts water to 1 part grain. Bring it to a boil, cover and simmer for 45 minutes.

BUCKWHEAT (Kasha)

This is actually a pyramid-shaped seed of a fruit rather than a true grain. Buckwheat has a rich and earthy flavor. Use it as a grain in cooked dishes. To prepare, dry roast it. You may coat the grains with a small amount of oil and stir while roasting. Then add boiling water, 2 parts water to 1 part grain. Cover and cook for 20 minutes.

BULGUR

Bulgur is cracked wheat that has been precooked and then dried. It has a nutty taste and fluffy texture. To prepare, add 2 parts boiling water to 1 part grain. Cover and let it stand for 20 minutes.

CORN

Corn kernels have a nutritional content similar to that of other grains. Cornmeal can be used to make cereals and muffins. Corn can be popped to produce popcorn.

MILLET

Millet is a delicate, nutty-tasting grain that looks like tiny yellow beads. Dry roasting or sautéing in oil is optional. To prepare, add 2 1/2 parts water to 1 part grain. Bring to a boil, cover and simmer for 30 minutes. Remove from the heat and uncover.

OATS

Oat flakes and oat bran, famous for their cholesterol-lowering action, can be used as a cereal and may be added to cookies, muffins, and breads. Rolled oats are used in granola mixes. To cook, add 3 parts boiling water to 1 part cereal. Simmer until done.

WHEAT BERRIES

Each berry is one whole wheat kernel. This is a very hard grain which, when cooked, has a chewy texture and a sweet flavor. Wheat berries may be sprouted, cracked, or eaten whole. To cook, add 3 parts water to 1 part grain. Bring to a boil, cover and simmer until done.

General cooking advice for grains:

Combine the grain and the boiling water, cover, reduce heat, and simmer.

An optional method that requires longer cooking times but produces a lighter product is as follows: Combine the grain and the boiling water and then bring the water again to a strong boil. Cover and turn off the heat. Allow the grain to stand covered for about 1 hour.

Note: Do not stir grains while cooking, as this makes them stick together.

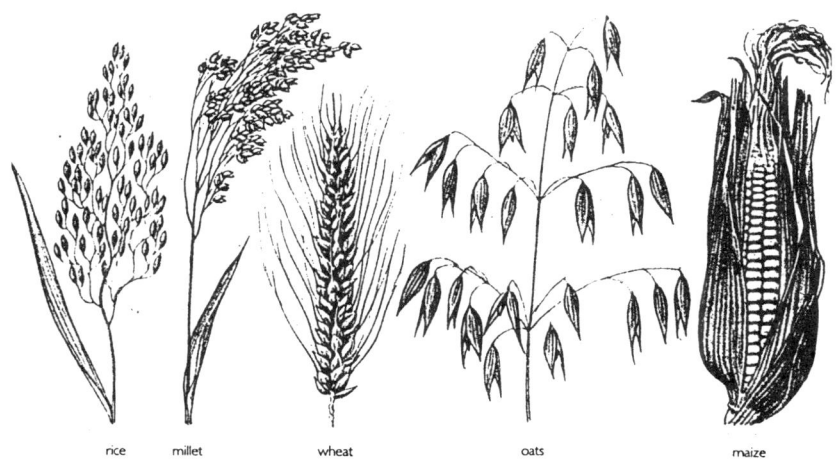

rice　　millet　　wheat　　oats　　maize

RECIPES

WHOLE-WHEAT BREAD

MAKES TWO 2-POUND (900 GRAM) LOAVES; 20 SLICES PER LOAF.
PREPARATION TIME 40 MINUTES. RISING TIME 90 MINUTES. BAKING TIME 50 MINUTES.

3 pounds (1.4 kg.) plain whole-wheat flour
2 teaspoons salt

1 ounce (40 g.) fresh yeast or 4 1/2 teaspoons dry yeast
2 teaspoons honey

Lightly oil and flour two 2-pound (900 g.) loaf tins and set aside. Put the flour and salt in a warmed bowl, mix well and set aside.

Blend the fresh yeast and the honey with 10 fluid ounces (300 ml.) of tepid water. If dry yeast is used, sprinkle it into 10 fluid ounces (300 ml.) of tepid water in which the honey has been blended, and leave this in a warm place for 15 minutes, until frothy.

Make a well in the center of the flour and pour in the yeast liquid. Mix well to form a firm dough, adding more tepid water as needed.

Cover the bowl containing the dough with a clean cloth. Leave it in a warm place for about 1 hour or until the dough has doubled in size.

To punch down the dough, turn it out onto a lightly floured surface and knead well for 10 minutes to remove any air bubbles. To knead, fold the dough in half. Lean into the dough using the palms of your hands. The pressure will flatten out the dough. Turn the dough a quarter turn, fold it in half, and continue kneading. Add small amounts of flour to your hands and to the board to prevent the dough from sticking. Divide into 2 equal pieces, then shape each into a loaf. Place in the loaf tins. Cover with a towel and leave in a warm place to rise for about 30 minutes, until the loaves have almost doubled in size.

Bake at 425°F (220°C) for 40-50 minutes, until baked through. The base of each loaf should sound hollow when gently tapped. Remove from the tins and cool on a rack.

WHOLE-WHEAT PITA BREAD

MAKES 8 PITAS. PREPARATION TIME 15 MINUTES.
RISING TIME 45 MINUTES. BAKING TIME 10 MINUTES.

1 pound (450 g.) plain whole-wheat flour

1 teaspoon dry yeast

1/4 teaspoon sea salt, optional
2 tablespoons olive oil
10 fluid ounces (300 ml.) tepid water

Lightly oil 1 or 2 baking sheets and set aside. Mix the whole-wheat flour, yeast, sea salt, and olive oil together, then add the water to make a soft but kneadable dough. Turn onto a well-floured work surface and knead for 8 minutes. Divide the dough into 8 pieces.

Using your palm, roll each piece of dough into a ball, and then, with a rolling pin, into an oval about 1/5 inch (1/2 cm.) thick.

Place on the baking sheet(s). Cover with a clean cloth and leave to rise in a warm place for about 45 minutes, until roughly doubled in size.

Bake at 450°F (230°C) for 10 minutes. Remove from the oven. To keep in the steam and create a soft bread, wrap well in a clean cloth or foil and set aside for at least 10 minutes. Before serving, place under a moderate grill to puff up.

KASHA VARNESHKAS

MAKES 8 CUPS. PREPARATION TIME 15 MINUTES. COOKING TIME 30 MINUTES.

1 package buckwheat kasha
2 cups whole-wheat noodles (bows or other shapes)

2 teaspoons oil
seasonings to taste (spices, sautéed onion, garlic)

Check kasha for stones, insects, and debris.

Put in a large pot. Add the oil to the dry kasha, and mix well. Stir over low heat until warm and slightly browned.

Pour in boiling water (3 times the amount of dry kasha), and bring to a quick boil. Season as desired. Turn off the heat and cover. Allow kasha to soak for about 30 minutes.

Cook the noodles separately in a generous amount of boiling water until soft. Strain, rinse, and mix well with the cooked kasha. Serve warm.

FRUIT CAKE

MAKES 2 CAKES. PREPARATION TIME 10 MINUTES. BAKING TIME 1 HOUR & 15 MINUTES.

2 cups whole-wheat flour
1 1/2 teaspoons baking powder
1 teaspoon baking soda
1/4 teaspoon cloves
1/2 teaspoon nutmeg
1/4 teaspoon allspice
1/2 teaspoon cinnamon

1-2 cups raisins or other dried fruits
1-1/2 cups water (360 ml.)
1/2 cup honey or fruit juice concentrate (120 ml.)
1/4 cup oil (60 ml.)
2 egg whites

Preheat the oven to 350°F (180°C). Oil 2 loaf pans.

Combine the dry ingredients by hand. Combine the liquid ingredients. Mix together.

Pour into loaf pans, and bake for 1 hour and 15 minutes.

BUBBY'S GRANOLA

MAKES ABOUT 5 CUPS. PREPARATION TIME 10 MINUTES. BAKING TIME 50 MINUTES.

2 1/2 cups regular rolled oats
1/2 cup slivered almonds
1/2 cup toasted wheat germ
1/2 cup sesame seeds

1/2 cup hulled sunflower seeds
1/2 cup honey
1/3 cup orange juice
1/2 cup raisins

In an extra-large mixing bowl combine the oats, almonds, wheat germ, sesame seeds, and sunflower seeds.

Stir together the honey and orange juice. Pour the mixture over the combined dry ingredients, stirring until evenly distributed. Spread the mixture evenly in a greased baking pan. Bake at 300°F (150°C) for 45-50 minutes or until brown, first stirring every 15 minutes, then several times during the last 15 minutes.

Remove from the oven. Stir in the raisins, transfer the mixture to another pan or bowl, and cool. Store in an airtight container up to 1 month.

TECHINA AND OATMEAL COOKIES

MAKES 30 COOKIES. PREPARATION TIME 10 MINUTES. BAKING TIME 15-30 MINUTES.

1/2 cup honey
1/2 cup chopped nuts
6 tablespoons techina
  (sesame butter)

1 teaspoon cinnamon
1 1/2 cups rolled oats
raisins, optional

Combine all the ingredients by hand.

Form little balls, and flatten with a fork dipped in water.

Bake on a greased cookie sheet in a 375°F (190°C) oven for 15-30 minutes until light brown. Do not overbake!

LEGUMES
(peas and beans)

AZUKI BEANS
CHICK-PEAS (Garbanzos)
LENTILS (brown, orange, green)
KIDNEY BEANS
MUNG BEANS
PEANUTS
SOYBEANS, SOY FLOUR, SOY MILK, TOFU
SPLIT PEAS (green, yellow)
WHITE BEANS (navy, lima)

QUALITIES AND PREPARATION OF LEGUMES

Beans and peas are a good source of protein and other nutrients. Eaten together with grains, they are an excellent substitute for meat (free of cholesterol and saturated fat) and are even effective in reducing bad LDL-cholesterol!

Use them for soups and stews and cook and sprinkle them on salads. Mash them after cooking for dips and sandwich spreads, and use them together with vegetables. Season them with garlic and onions or add herbs or spices.

To remove the gas-producing, undigestive carbohydrate that sticks to the outer skin of legumes, soak the peas or beans overnight in the refrigerator in a bowl of water. Rinse and then cook in fresh water. Legumes must be boiled in plenty of water for a long period of time — at least 1 1/2 hours — until soft. It's a good idea to begin with small servings of legumes and increase amounts gradually, thereby allowing your body to produce the digestive enzymes needed to properly digest beans and peas.

CHICK-PEAS (Garbanzo Beans)

These are large, round, beige beans with a nutty taste. Use chick-peas in salads, soups, and as a spread.

LENTILS

These come in several varieties as small brown-, orange-, or green-colored beans. Use them in soups or salads. They can also be mixed with grains. Lentils do not need pre-soaking.

KIDNEY BEANS

These beans are red and kidney-shaped. Use them in salads, stews, and soups.

SOYBEANS

These are small, yellow beans that contain more protein than any other vegetable source. Soy products, which are more easily digestible than the beans alone, include soy flour, soy milk, soy sauce, and tofu (bean curd or soy cheese).

SPLIT PEAS

Split peas have a hearty flavor and come in green and yellow varieties. They taste great in soups or may be eaten with whole grains. Split peas do not need pre-soaking.

WHITE BEANS

These are white, middle-sized beans. Use them in stews, salads, and soups. They combine nicely with tomatoes or with tomato sauce and herbs.

RECIPES

LENTIL SOUP

MAKES 3 CUPS. PREPARATION TIME 10 MINUTES. COOKING TIME 1-1 1/2 HOURS.

1 cup lentils
4 cups water
3 cloves garlic, minced

1 onion, grated
salt
coriander

Combine the ingredients in a large pot and bring to a boil. Skim the foam.

Simmer until lentils are soft (about 1 1/4 hours).

BEAN SALAD

MAKES 10 SERVINGS. PREPARATION TIME 5 MINUTES. MARINATION TIME 3-6 HOURS.

2 cups cooked green beans
2 cups cooked yellow beans
2 cups cooked chick-peas
1 pound (1/2 kg.) cooked red kidney beans, optional

1 onion, sliced thin
1/4 cup oil
1/2 cup vinegar
1/3 cup honey
1 teaspoon salt

Place the beans and the chick-peas in a large bowl and add the sliced onion.

Separately, combine the remaining ingredients and pour over the vegetables, mixing well.

Refrigerate several hours or overnight.

Natural cooking

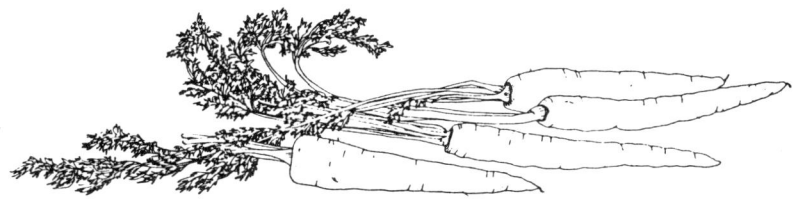

VEGETABLES (raw or cooked)		
Artichokes	Horseradish	Pumpkin
Asparagus	Kale	Radishes
Beets	Kohlrabi	Red cabbage
Broccoli	Leeks	Scallions
Cabbage	Lettuce	Spinach
Carrots	Mint	Sprouts (all kinds)
Cauliflower	Mushrooms	Squashes
Celery	Onions	String beans
Corn	Parsley	Sweet potatoes
Cucumbers	Parsnips	Tomatoes
Eggplant	Peppers	Turnips
Garlic	Potatoes	

Vegetables are an important source of vitamins and minerals. They are especially good sources of vitamins A and C and supply, as well, riboflavin, folacin, iron, and magnesium. Due to their high fiber content, vegetables are filling while remaining low in calories.

STEAMING VEGETABLES

Steam vegetables to retain their color and texture, and their water-soluble vitamins. Put the vegetables on a stainless-steel steamer above 1-2 inches (2-4 cm.) of water in a covered saucepan. Bring the water to a boil and reduce the heat. Steam covered for the least amount of time necessary, which varies according to the type of vegetable being prepared.

RECIPES

CARROT TZIMMES

MAKES 5 SERVINGS. PREPARATION TIME 15 MINUTES. COOKING TIME 1 HOUR.

5 large carrots, peeled *1 tablespoon oil*
orange juice to cover *10 small prunes*
2 tablespoons honey *dash of ginger, optional*

Slice the carrots, cover with orange juice in a small pot, and boil for about 10 minutes.

Add the honey, oil, and whole prunes.

Simmer over a low fire for about 1 hour, or until most of the liquid is absorbed.

Add ginger if desired, and simmer a few minutes more.

BEET BORSCHT

MAKES 8 SERVINGS. PREPARATION TIME 10 MINUTES. COOKING TIME 1 HOUR.

8 large beets *1/4 cup lemon juice*
2 quarts (2 liters) water *2 tablespoons honey*
2 teaspoons salt *or fruit juice concentrate*

Peel the beets. Cut, dice or grate them.

Combine the beets, water, salt, and honey or fruit juice concentrate, and cook for 1 hour.

Add the lemon juice.

Chill and serve.

Natural cooking

CHREIN

MAKES ABOUT 2 1/2 CUPS. PREPARATION TIME 5 MINUTES.

2 cups boiled beets, grated *1/2 cup grated*
1/2 cup vinegar *fresh horseradish*

Blend all the ingredients in a blender.
Refrigerate.

VEGETABLE SOUP

MAKES 5 SERVINGS. PREPARATION TIME 10 MINUTES. COOKING TIME 30 MINUTES.

4 potatoes, peeled *1 onion*
3 carrots, peeled *1 bunch parsley or dill*
2 squash *2 cloves garlic*
2 stalks celery *salt, to taste*

Blend all the ingredients in a blender.

Put in a large pot, add enough water to cover vegetables, cover and cook 1/2 hour.

SPROUTS

Each sprout is both a small leafy vegetable and a bean or seed. It contains protein, carbohydrates, vitamins — especially A, B, C, and E — and minerals. Use alfalfa seeds, mung beans, lentils, soybeans, wheat berries, or sunflower seeds to make your sprouts. The only equipment you really need is a flat baking dish covered with a towel. Sprouts will provide you with variety in eating. Their proteins are in a simpler form than those in the unsprouted beans or seeds and are therefore more digestible.

MAKING SPROUTS

Day 1

Soak 1/4 cup seeds or beans in 1 cup of water in a dish or a jar for at least 10 hours.

Day 2

Drain the water from the seeds or beans and rinse well with cold water. Place them in a single layer on a wide flat dish. Cover with a damp layer of paper towels; cover the dish with a towel. (Alternate method: Place the seeds or beans in a jar. Cover the mouth of the jar with cheesecloth attached with a rubber band or with a sprouting lid. Wrap the jar in a towel and rest it on its side.)

Rinse the seeds or beans thoroughly twice a day with cool water. After rinsing, cover the seeds or beans, in a dish, with a paper towel and a dish towel.

Days 3-5

Continue rinsing twice a day. Most sprouts will be ready by day 4. The sprouts should be at least 2-3 times the length of the initial seed or bean.

Refrigerate in plastic bags for up to a week. Daily rinsing of sprouts with cool water, allowing all the water to drain off, will preserve their freshness and will extend their storage life.

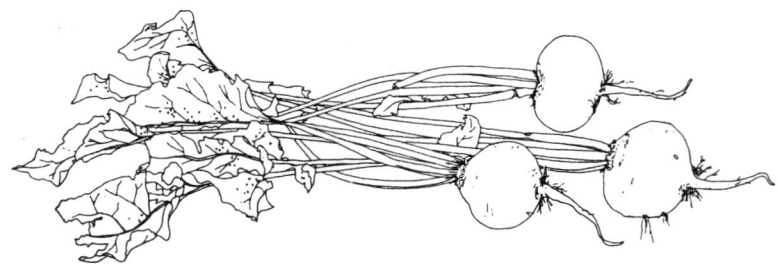

FRUITS

FRESH FRUITS

Apples	Guava	Papaya
Apricots	Kiwi	Peaches
Bananas	Kumquats	Pears
Berries	Lemons	Persimmons
Cactus	Loquats	Pineapple
Cherries	Mandarin oranges	Plums
Dates	Mango	Pomegranates
Figs	Melons	Strawberries
Grapefruit	Nectarines	Tangerines
Grapes	Oranges	Watermelon

DRIED FRUITS

Apricots	Figs	Prunes
Dates	Papaya	Raisins

FRUIT JUICES

Apple	Grapefruit	Peach
Apricot	Mango	Pineapple
Grape	Orange	Prune

Fruits are excellent sources of vitamins A and C, fiber, and potassium. They can be consumed raw, as juice, dried, lightly cooked, or even baked. Choose from a wide variety as they appear in their seasons, and enjoy!

RECIPES

APPLE COMPOTE

MAKES 4 SERVINGS. PREPARATION TIME 10 MINUTES. COOKING TIME 30 MINUTES.

1 pound (1/2 kg.) apples *juice of 1 lemon*
2 cups water *cinnamon or cloves, optional*
2 tablespoons honey

Peel, core and cut the apples as desired, in bite-size pieces or sliced.

Put the apples and water in a pot, and bring to a boil. Simmer covered for 1/2 hour.

Add the honey, lemon juice, and spices.

Chill and serve.

FRUIT SALAD

MAKES 6 SERVINGS. PREPARATION TIME 10 MINUTES.

3 oranges *juice of 1 lemon*
4 bananas *cloves or mint, optional*
3 apples *honey or fruit juice*
raisins or chopped dates *concentrate, optional*

Peel and slice the oranges and bananas; cut up the apples after washing well.

Add the raisins or chopped dates, and the lemon juice.

If desired, add honey or fruit juice concentrate and spices, to taste.

Mix well, chill, and serve.

FRUIT BARS

MAKES 8 BARS. PREPARATION TIME 25 MINUTES. BAKING TIME 50 MINUTES.

1 pound (450 g.) apples, peeled, cored and finely chopped

2 ounces (60 g.) dried apricots, rinsed and chopped

2 ounces (60 g.) raisins, rinsed

2 1/2 ounces (75 g.) rolled oats

2 1/2 ounces (75 g.) whole-meal flour

2 teaspoons baking powder

2 ounces (60 g.) pitted dates, rinsed and coarsely chopped

3 ounces (90 g.) mixed nuts, chopped

1 ounce (30 g.) sesame seeds

1 ounce (30 g.) pumpkin seeds

6 tablespoons unsweetened apple juice

3 tablespoons oil

Lightly grease a 7 inch (18 cm.) square tin.

Put the apples in a heavy-based saucepan with 1 tablespoon of water. Cover tightly and cook for about 10 minutes, until the apples are very soft.

Uncover and continue to cook the apples, stirring, for an additional 2 minutes or until the excess moisture has evaporated.

Add the remaining ingredients and mix together well.

Pack into the prepared tin and level the surface. Bake at 325°F (170°C) on a low shelf in the oven, for 30-40 minutes. Move the tin to the top of the oven for another 10 minutes of baking time. When completely baked, the mixture will be slightly brown around the edges and will feel firm to the touch.

Mark into 8 bars while still warm. Leave to cool in the tin. When cold, turn out and cut into bars.

APPLESAUCE (NO SUGAR ADDED)

MAKES 3 CUPS. PREPARATION TIME 10 MINUTES. COOKING TIME 10 MINUTES.

2 pounds (1 kg.) apples, unpeeled

1/2 teaspoon cinnamon, optional

1/2 cup apple or pineapple juice

Wash the apples well, cut into small pieces, and place in a large pot.

Add the juice and, if desired, cinnamon, and bring to a boil.

Cover pot and cook 10 minutes over a medium fire, then cool. Mash to desired consistency or process in a blender or food mill.

Serve chilled.

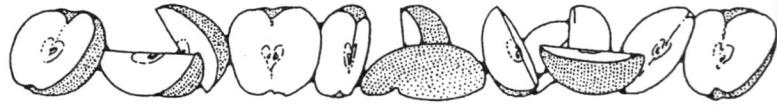

ANIMAL PRODUCTS

Fish is considered a healthy food by many researchers. Fish oils include omega-3, which may be a protective factor against heart disease. Several fish meals per week, not fried, may be included as part of a healthy diet.

Two to three servings of milk or milk products per day are generally recommended. These should be as low in fat as possible, ideally consisting of skim, 1/2%, or 1% milk, yogurt, or cheese.

Lean meats and poultry, if eaten, should be consumed only in limited amounts, generally with the skin and extra fat removed, and not fried.

Egg yolks, which are high in cholesterol, should be limited and eaten only on occasion. The whites, however, which contain no fat or cholesterol, may be eaten unrestrictedly and may be used in cooking and baking.

RECIPES

CHAMIN — "MACHSHI"

A TASTY SEPHARDIC COOKED DISH FOR THE SHABBOS MORNING MEAL.
MAKES 6 SERVINGS. PREPARATION TIME 30 MINUTES. COOKING TIME 2 HOURS.

10 small, finger-size squash, sliced	2 quinces (if available), sliced, optional
2 cups uncooked rice	1 apple, peeled and sliced
2 tomatoes, chopped	3-4 dates, pitted
1 onion	juice of 1 lemon
2 beets, sliced	2 tablespoons tomato paste
1 chicken, cut into eighths	seasonings (paprika, salt, black pepper), optional

Cut off the stems of the squash; carve out the inside seeds and pulp, and reserve.

Brown the onions in a frying pan with little or no oil.

Prepare a mixture of the raw rice, chopped tomatoes, browned onions, and seasonings (to taste). Fill each hollowed squash with this mixture.

Put the seeds and pulp of the squash in a large pot, covering the bottom. Over this, spread a layer of beet slices; then place the cut and cleaned chicken (after removing the skin and fat). Arrange the stuffed squash on top of the chicken; and over the squash, spread the apples, quinces, dates, lemon juice, and tomato paste. Add enough water to cover the entire mixture.

Cover the pot, bring it to a boil, and cook 2 hours over a low fire. Transfer it to an electric Shabbos hotplate to keep it warm until the Shabbos morning meal.

LIGHT CHOLENT

MAKES 6 SERVINGS. PREPARATION TIME 20 MINUTES. COOKING TIME 2 HOURS.

1 small chicken, cut into serving portions

8 potatoes

1 onion

2 garlic cloves

1 cup white beans, soaked over-night, or 1 cup barley, optional

mushrooms, optional

seasonings (salt, pepper, etc.)

2 tablespoons tomato paste, optional

Peel the potatoes, onion, and garlic.

Put them in a large pot together with the cleaned and skinned chicken (remove all visible fat), the optional ingredients, and seasonings (to taste), and cover with water.

Cover the pot, bring to a boil, and simmer over a low flame for 2 hours. Transfer it to an electric Shabbos hotplate to keep it warm until the Shabbos morning meal.

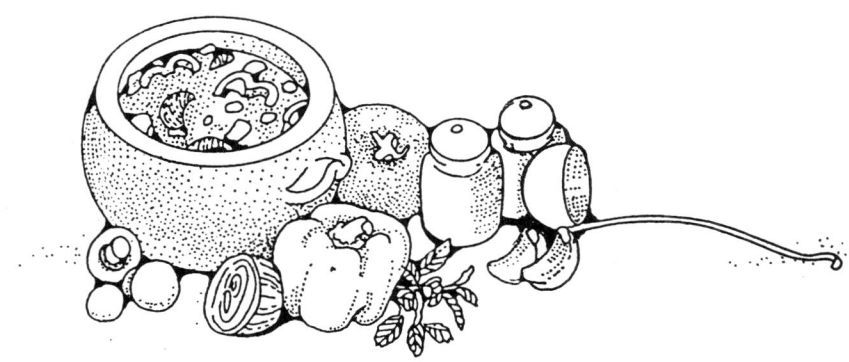

OILS

We must consume a limited amount of fat on a regular basis in order to obtain fat-soluble vitamins and the essential linoleic fatty acid. The oils most recommended are cold-pressed olive or canola, as these are highest in monounsaturated fats, which today are considered the most heart-healthy. About a tablespoon or two per day is all we need. Large amounts of even these healthy oils may have detrimental effects on our blood cholesterol levels. Alternative oils which may be used on occasion include safflower, corn, soy, sunflower, and sesame. With these oils, as well, the cold-pressed varieties are recommended, as the heat extract method converts these oils to a less healthy form.

Nuts are very high in fat and therefore do not have much of a place in this diet. They should be eaten only in limited amounts on rare occasions. There are some seeds, however, which may be used to add variety, texture, and flavor: poppy seeds, sesame seeds, sunflower seeds, and sprouted seeds.

SAUCES, DRESSINGS, AND TOPPINGS

Sauces are traditionally high in fat, made with plenty of butter, flour, oil, and eggs. Alternative ideas, using healthier thickening agents — such as cornstarch, whole-grain flours, and pureed vegetables and legumes — will add variety and palatability to your vegetables and grains. A successful sauce or dressing can turn a plain salad, or fruit, grain or pasta dish into a gourmet's delight and can be the saving factor for many in the pursuit of a healthy nutritional lifestyle.

RECIPES

HIGH-CALCIUM HALVAH BAR

THIS RECIPE CONTAINS ABOUT 400 MILLIGRAMS OF CALCIUM.
MAKES A ONE OUNCE BAR. PREPARATION TIME 5 MINUTES.

1 tablespoon carob powder

1/2 teaspoon water

sesame seeds or wheat germ

2 teaspoons blackstrap molasses

2 tablespoons sesame butter (from whole ground seeds)

Combine all the ingredients and stir well.

Roll the mixture into a bar and coat with whole sesame seeds or wheat germ.

Serve at room temperature or frozen.

TOMATO SAUCE (for grain, pasta, and vegetable dishes)

MAKES 3 CUPS. PREPARATION TIME 20 MINUTES.

2 cloves garlic, finely minced

1 onion, finely grated

2 teaspoons oil, preferably cold-pressed

1 pound (1/2 kg.) pureed ripe tomatoes, fresh or canned

1 cup water

4 teaspoons fresh or 2 teaspoons dried herbs (i.e., oregano, basil, thyme)

Lightly sauté the onion and garlic in oil.

Add the tomatoes and water, stir well, and simmer for several minutes.

Add the herbs and simmer for a few more minutes.

GRAVY

MAKES 6 CUPS. PREPARATION TIME 20 MINUTES.

*2 pounds (1 kg.) vegetables
(potato, carrots, squash, etc.)*
2 cups soup stock or water
*1 tablespoon whole-wheat flour,
lightly browned, or cornstarch*
1 onion, grated
3 cloves garlic, minced

*optional:
vinegar
tomato puree
mushrooms
dry wine
lemon
honey
herbs or spices*

Cook the vegetables in a large pot in a small amount of water until tender. Mash the vegetables by hand or process them in a blender.

Add enough liquid so as to achieve a satisfactory consistency, along with the flour or cornstarch. Add the onion and garlic.

Add any of the optional ingredients. If desired, they may first be lightly sautéed in oil.

Cook the mixture for several minutes, while stirring. Serve over grains, pastas, or vegetables. Experiment and enjoy!

LOW-FAT SALAD DRESSING

MAKES 1 CUP. PREPARATION TIME 10 MINUTES.

2 tablespoons oil, preferably cold-pressed
juice of 1 lemon
3 tablespoons cider vinegar
1 clove garlic, minced
1/2 cup water
1-2 teaspoons dried or fresh herbs, chopped (i.e., basil, dill, marjoram, parsley)

optional:
onion, minced
1 ripe tomato, grated
additional garlic, minced
additional lemon juice
addtional herbs or spices

Shake the ingredients in a tightly closed glass bottle (or blend in a food processor) before serving.

The mixture may be stored several days in the refrigerator.

FRUIT TOPPING

MAKES 4 CUPS. PREPARATION TIME 15-25 MINUTES.

2 pounds (1 kg.) ripe fruit, pitted and sliced
1 cup water

1/4-1/3 cup honey or fruit juice concentrate
cloves, cinnamon, mint, etc., optional

Place the fruit and water in a saucepan, stir, and bring to a boil.

Add the honey or fruit juice concentrate, spices and herbs, stir, and simmer covered for several minutes.

To thicken the mixture, let it stand covered for several hours. Then cook it again over a medium fire and stir to thicken it further. One tablespoon of cornstarch dissolved in 2 tablespoons of cold water may be added, also, as a thickening agent.

3 | Seasoning with spices and herbs

Spices and herbs include a great variety of vegetable products with aromatic odors and pungent flavors that can enhance the natural flavor of foods. They may be used to add variety and improve the taste of your meals when fat and salt must be controlled, in preparing special diets. A pinch of herbs and a dash of imagination can turn everyday foods into culinary delights!

Spices are defined as parts of plants — such as the dried seeds, buds, fruit or flower parts, or the bark or roots of plants — usually of tropical origin. Herbs are from the leafy parts of temperate-zone plants.

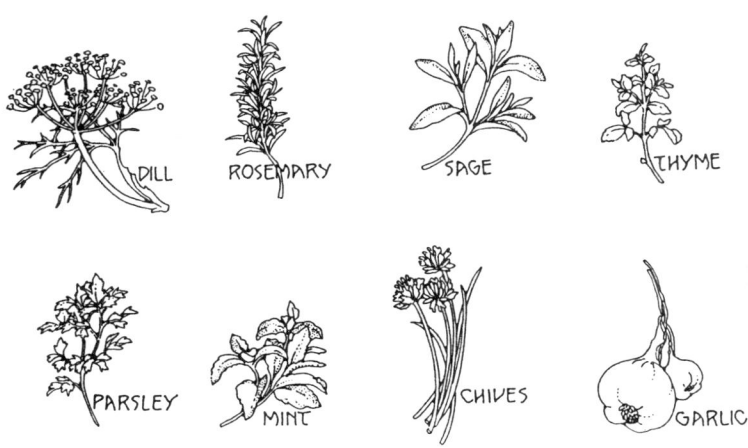

GROUPS OF SPICES AND HERBS

LEAVES

basil	dill weed	rosemary
bay leaf	marjoram	sage
chervil	mint	savory
chives	oregano	tarragon
coriander (cilantro)	parsley	thyme

FRUITS

allspice	clove	red pepper
black pepper	mace	vanilla bean
caper	paprika	white pepper

SEEDS

anise	coriander seed	mustard
caraway	cumin	nutmeg
cardamom	dill seed	poppy seed
celery seed	fennel	sesame seed
	fenugreek	

BULBS AND ROOTS

garlic	ginger	turmeric
	onion	

BARK

cinnamon (cassia)

The above chart is a partial listing of spices and herbs prepared by the U.S. Department of Agriculture, Washington, D.C.

A few spices — celery seed, cumin, coriander leaf, dill weed, cloves, and especially parsley flakes — are very high in sodium

(3-9 mg. per 2 g.). Their use may be contraindicated in therapeutic diets in which sodium (salt) is highly restricted.

Herbal hints

Spices and herbs should be stored in a cool, dry place in airtight containers. Chop, cut or crush fresh herbs to release their flavors. Experiment with herbs by increasing the amount to suit your personal taste.

Generally, if a recipe is not available, one should start with 1/8 of a teaspoon of powdered herbs, 1/4 of a teaspoon of dried herbs or 1 teaspoon of chopped, fresh herbs when preparing a dish that makes 4 to 6 servings.

Never use herbs to season every dish at one meal. It is better to use caution and start with limited amounts of herbs and spices, until you are familiar with their powers, rather than take a reckless approach.

The best cooks use herbs with discretion. They must be used sparingly or they will overpower, rather than enhance, the natural flavors of foods.

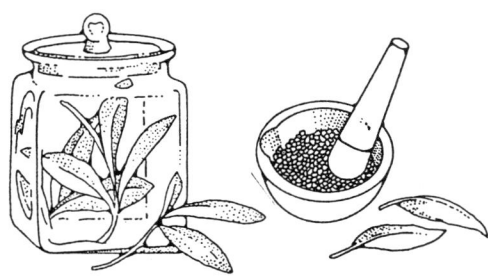

Suggestions for using herbs and spices

Below are suggestions for the successful use of herbs and spices in daily cooking, so as to achieve gourmet flavor.

Anise seed	cookies, cakes, breads, candy, cheese, beverages, pickles, beef stew, stewed fruits, fish.
Basil	tomatoes, noodles, rice, beef stew, meat loaf, fish, vegetable salad, eggplant, potatoes, eggs, carrots, spinach, peas, cheese, jelly.
Bay leaf	soups, pickles, fish, meat roasts.
Caraway seed	green beans, beets, cabbage, carrots, cauliflower, potatoes, sauerkraut, turnips, zucchini, beef stew, cake, cookies, rice, rye bread.
Celery seed	potato salad, fruit salad, tomatoes, vegetables, pickles, breads, rolls, egg dishes, meat loaf, stews, soups.
Cinnamon	beverages, bakery products, fruits, pickles, beef stews, roast chicken.
Cloves	fruits, pickles, baked goods, fish, meat sauces, pot roast, green beans, carrots, sweet potatoes, tomatoes.
Dill seed	pickles, pickled beets, salads, sauerkraut, green beans, egg dishes, stews, fish, chicken, breads.

Seasoning with spices and herbs

Fennel seed	egg dishes, fish, stews, cheese, vegetables, baked apples, pickles, sauerkraut, breads, cakes, cookies.
Garlic	tomato dishes, soups, dips, sauces, salads, pickles, meat, poultry, fish, bread.
Ginger	pickles, baked fruits, soups, vegetables, baked products, beef, poultry, fish, beverages.
Marjoram	beef, poultry, fish, tomato dishes, carrots, peas, spinach, squash, mushrooms, broccoli, pizza, spaghetti, egg dishes, breads, soups.
Mint	punches, tea, vegetables, sauces for desserts.
Mustard seed	pickles, potato salad, cabbage, sauerkraut.
Nutmeg	hot beverages, puddings, baked products, fruits, chicken, eggs, vegetables, pickles.
Onion	dips, soups, stews, meats, fish, poultry, salads, vegetables, cheese dishes, egg dishes, breads, rice dishes.
Oregano	tomatoes, pasta sauces, pizza, vegetable soup, egg dishes, cheese dishes, onions, chicken, fish.

Paprika	beef, poultry, fish, egg dishes, cheese dishes, vegetables lacking in color, pickles.
Parsley	soups, breads, tomato and meat sauces, broiled or fried fish, meats, poultry.
Pepper, black	meats, poultry, fish, eggs, vegetables, pickles.
Pepper, white	white or light meats, vegetables.
Poppy seed	pie crust, scrambled eggs, fruit compotes, cookies, cakes, breads, noodles. Sprinkle on top of fruit, salads, breads, vegetables, cookies, and cakes.
Rosemary	beef, poultry, fish, soups, potatoes, cauliflower, spinach, mushrooms, turnips, fruits, breads.
Sage	beef, poultry, fish, cheese, sauces, onions, eggplant, lima beans, tomatoes, soups, potatoes.
Sesame seed	pies, cakes, cookies, dips. Sprinkle on breads, cookies, salads, noodles, soups, and vegetables.
Thyme	meat, poultry, fish, vegetables.
Vanilla	baked goods, beverages, puddings.

PART III:
The Spiritual Effects of Eating

A physician restricts the diet of only those patients whom he expects to recover. So God prescribed dietary laws for those who have hope of a future life.

R. Tanchum ben Chanilai, Vayikra Rabbah 13:2

1 | Spirituality of eating*

Why do we eat?

When asked why they eat, people usually respond, "I eat because I'm hungry," "I eat when something looks or smells good," or "I eat because it's meal time." For many, the routine of eating is an agony to minimize or avoid by skipping breakfast or using instant powders or fast foods. Others snack through the day without ever sitting down to a meal! In this chapter we shall examine what really happens when we eat — from both spiritual and physical points of view.

In the beginning

To achieve historical perspective, we must go back in time to the beginning, to the Garden of Eden and the Tree of Knowledge.

> God took the man and put him into the Garden of Eden to work it and keep it. God commanded the man, saying, "You may freely eat from every tree of the garden. But from the Tree of Knowledge of good and evil do not eat, for on the day you eat from it, you will surely die" [*Bereshis* 2:15-17].

If only the first man, Adam, had kept on occupying himself

---

* The author is grateful to "Shamir" (the Association of Religious Professionals from the Soviet Union and Eastern Europe in Israel), which originally published this chapter in its publication *B'Or Ha'Torah* (no. 8, 1993).

with Torah and with guarding the way to the Tree of Life, he would have continued to stroll through the Garden of Eden like one of the guardian angels. Shortly after God created Chavah, in the afternoon of the first Friday of Creation, the first couple in the world committed the first sin by eating the forbidden fruit of the Tree of Knowledge of good and evil. If they had only waited a few hours for Shabbos, they could have eaten the fruit with God's blessings! (*Shaar ha-Kavanos, Rosh Hashanah*, Discourse A).

Likewise, we read in the *Chumash*:

> The woman saw that the tree was good for food and desirable to the eyes, and the tree was attractive as a means to gain intelligence. She took some of its fruit and ate, and also gave some to her husband, and he ate [*Bereshis* 3:6].

The trees were real trees, the fruits were real fruits, and the eating was actual eating; but the fruits were fine and the eating was delicate. As the Ramchal (Rabbi Moshe Chayim Luzzatto) explains in *Da'as Tevunos*, the eating from the Tree of Knowledge introduced desire for all material, bodily pleasures and for all sins.

In the beginning, good and evil had been separate, both in the fruit and in the entire world. But when the sin of the Tree of Knowledge corrupted the world, good became mixed with evil. Sparks of holiness fell into their husks, and the pure combined with the impure. Man was sentenced to work hard for his food and to die. The world became more coarse.

Eat with caution

In *Tanna d'Vei Eliyahu*, the prophet Eliyahu is claimed to acrimoniously blame all our troubles on eating:

> I call heaven and earth to bear witness that all the children of man are gathered to death and all creatures descend to sorrow only because of eating and drinking [*Eliyahu Zuta* 3].

The commentary *Zikkukin d'Nura* explains that all sins result from overindulging in food and drink. We learn in the Torah that satiation leads to forgetting or even rejecting God.

> You may eat and be satisfied....But your heart might grow haughty, and you might forget your God, Who brought you out of Egypt, the house of slavery [*Devarim* 8:12-14].

> For this reason we are commanded not to eat on Yom Kippur, the day of atonement for our sins, since improper eating has the power to turn our souls to wrongdoing [Rabbenu Bachya, *Shulchan shel Arba'ah*].

Hunger and appetite mechanisms

Hunger is defined as an uneasy sensation caused by want of food. Appetite is the complex of sensations by which an organism is aware of its desire for food. The physical basis of hunger is regulated by the "feeding center" in the hypothalamic portion of the brain. The appetite-regulating mechanism in a normal human being adjusts food intake to the point where caloric intake balances the output of energy. This maintains body weight.

Thirst, the desire to drink, is regulated by the hypothalamic osmoreceptors of the brain. A dry sensation in the mouth also motivates a person to drink.

The physical basis of hunger and thirst has been well proven. However, the psychological motivating factors are often the overriding influence driving one to eat or drink too much. Most habitual eating is unrelated to hunger. It is more related to one's surroundings, including the presence or reminders of food, or to one's emotional state. In short, we often eat for many reasons besides that of satisfying our physical need for food!

Components of food

It is clear that the soul is not nourished by physical bread, as the body is. The food we eat is actually a combination of both a physical and a spiritual entity. The body is nourished by the physical aspects, or nutrients, contained in the foods we eat; the soul is nourished by the spiritual power — or sparks of holiness — which enlivens the physical substance of all matter, including food. Therefore, body and soul are united in the act of eating (*Ruach Chayim* on *Pirkei Avos* 3:3; *Shulchan Aruch, Orach Chayim* 6:1, and see *Magen Avraham* on verse 4 there).

We have seen that all of Creation is composed of a mixture of good and evil. Likewise, in every food that a person eats there is a combination of good and evil. Food physically consists of good counterparts, i.e., nutrients, and bad aspects, i.e., waste or undigestible matter. Likewise, spiritually, food contains sparks of holiness, or good components, and husks, or *kelipos*, which are the gross, bad components that encompass the sparks.

Physical origins: the nutrients

Where does food come from? Plants grow by effectively combining sunlight, water, and soil. Animals feed on plants and/or animals. Humans obtain their food from mineral, vegetable, and animal sources.

Nutrients, which are contained in our food, must be consumed in adequate amounts in order to grow. In the body, these nutrients are converted to thousands of substances which contribute to healthy living.

Nutrients, as noted early in this book, are divided into six general classes: carbohydrates, fats, proteins, vitamins, minerals, and water.

Spiritual origins: the sparks — *Shechinah*, manna, food

Before descending into the body, the soul is nourished as the angels are — directly through the radiance of the *Shechinah* (the Divine Presence). Separated by the body from its former supernal nourishment, the soul now is nourished by physical food (which is the manifestation of that Divine nourishment). Thus, when one eats, one benefits somewhat from the radiance of the *Shechinah* (*Reshis Chachmah, Sha'ar ha-Kedushah*

15:51; *Siddur Tefillah l'Moshe,* edited by the Ramak [see his commentary on *"Elokay Neshamah"*]).

> The soul, clothed in the physical garment of the flesh, is now nourished indirectly by God through food. Such is God's Will, that we should exist with our physical limitations, and that we should require physical food to sustain our vital forces. Only in the future world, when stripped of its physical garment, will food become recognizable as radiance of the Divine Presence. However, in this world it appears clothed in its physical garment [*Peri Tzaddik, "Es ha-Ochel"*].
>
> Food, then, comes into the world from the supernal table of Heaven [*Reshis Chachmah, Sha'ar ha-Kedushah* 15:46].
>
> ...The sin of eating from the Tree of Knowledge caused good to become mixed with evil throughout the world and sparks of holiness to fall amidst the husks. These sparks of holiness are scattered throughout Creation and are contained in varying amounts in the food we eat. These sparks of holiness give plants the strength to emerge and grow from the soil as they are watered by the rains [*Yesod v'Shoresh ha-Avodah, sha'ar* 7, ch. 1].

After the Jews were redeemed from slavery in Egypt, they ate manna in the desert for forty years. Manna is not ordinary coarse food but, rather, a physical form of supernal light. It descended daily and, unlike all other foods, was completely absorbed into the body when eaten.

> ...In the morning, there was a layer of dew around the camp. When the layer of dew evaporated, the desert was covered with flakes like fine frost on the ground. The Israelites saw it and asked one another, "What is it? (*Man hu?*)" because they didn't know what it was, and Moshe said to them, "This is the bread that God has given you to eat" [*Shemos* 16:13-15].
>
> The House of Israel called it manna (*man*). It looked like coriander seed [except that it was] white. It tasted like a honey wafer [*Shemos* 16:31].

Manna descended from Heaven completely good, with no mixture of evil, since no evil descends from Heaven. Therefore, it contained no waste and was absorbed completely [*Ruach Chayim* on *Pirkei Avos* 3].

The manna and the fruits of the Garden of Eden were similar in that they were both completely absorbed into the limbs of the body [Ramban, *Bereshis* 2:17].

Combination of Good and Evil in Our Foods		
	Spiritual Aspects (*Soul*)	*Physical Aspects* (*Body*)
GOOD	Sparks	Nutrients
EVIL	Husks	Waste

Digestion of food

Food is first introduced into the mouth, where it is chewed by the teeth in order to break up large food particles to mix it with saliva, thus beginning the process known as digestion. The food is then propelled into the esophagus by the tongue with the aid of the swallowing mechanism. The food travels down the esophagus until it reaches the stomach. Food is stored in the stomach, mixed with acid and other digestive juices, and released at a controlled, steady rate into the entrance of the small intestine, where it is digested further and absorbed. In the small intestine, the intestinal contents are mixed with pancreatic juice, bile, and other secretions.

The intestinal contents continue down the long, winding tube of the small intestine until they pass into the thick tube of the large intestine, the main function of which is to absorb water, salt and other minerals, and certain vitamins. Stool containing inorganic (non-carbon-containing) material, undigested plant fibers, bacteria, and water is excreted from the body through the rectum.

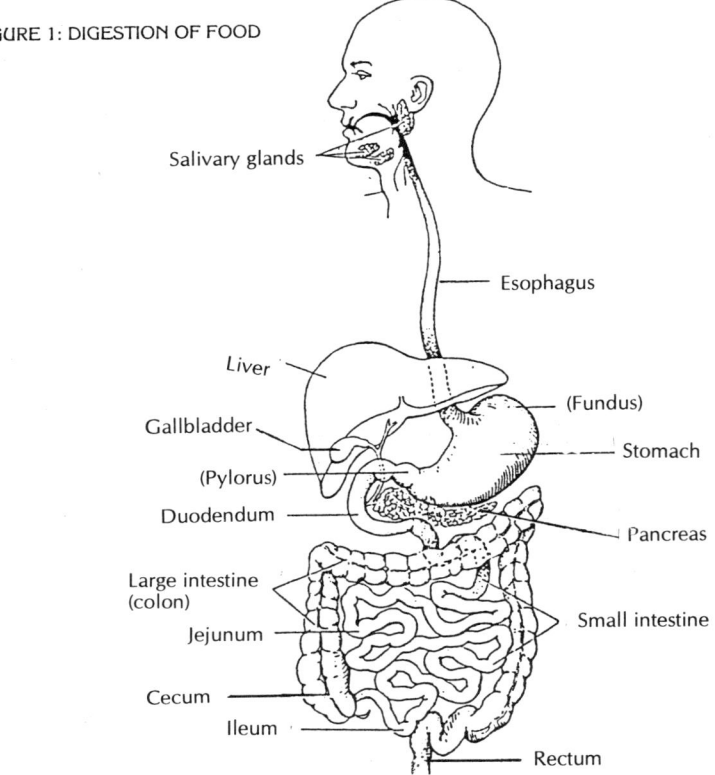

FIGURE 1: DIGESTION OF FOOD

Absorption of Food

Although limited amounts of water, alcohol, simple salts, and glucose are absorbed through the stomach wall, the small intestine is by far the most important organ for absorption. Absorption into the small intestine consists primarily of the transfer of nutrients from the interior (lumen) of the small intestine through the cells lining the intestinal wall into the wall of the small intestine (the lamina propria). From there the nutrients enter the blood and lymph vessels. The nutrients are then carried to all parts of the body through the bloodstream. The waste materials are eliminated from the body via stool, urine, sweat, and expired air. The small intestine, then, is the main site of selection of the nutrients for use in the body, leaving the waste for eventual elimination.

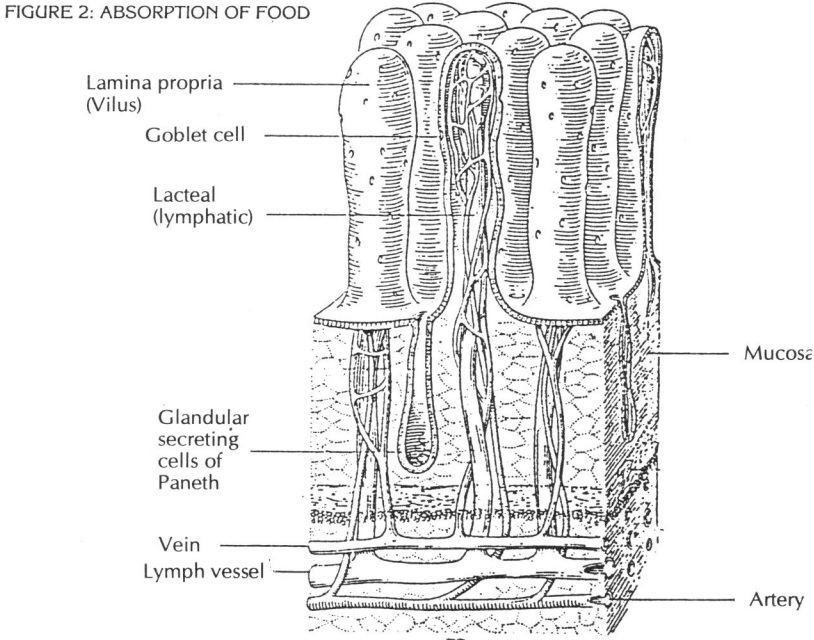

FIGURE 2: ABSORPTION OF FOOD

Lamina propria (Vilus)
Goblet cell
Lacteal (lymphatic)
Glandular secreting cells of Paneth
Vein
Lymph vessel
Mucosa
Artery

Use of the Nutrients

The end products of the digestive processes discussed are amino acids of proteins, fat derivatives, and simple carbohydrates. These compounds are absorbed and metabolized in the body by various routes. The intricate details of their metabolism are studied by biochemists.

How do we get energy from the food we eat? The derivation of energy from a physical source is the most spiritual of our bodily processes. To function properly the body must be constantly supplied with fuel or energy, supplied by either digesting food or drawing on its fat stores when adequate food is not available. The chemical energy which derives from this as well as all life processes is held in the high-energy bonds of adenosine triphosphate (ATP), found in all forms of life.

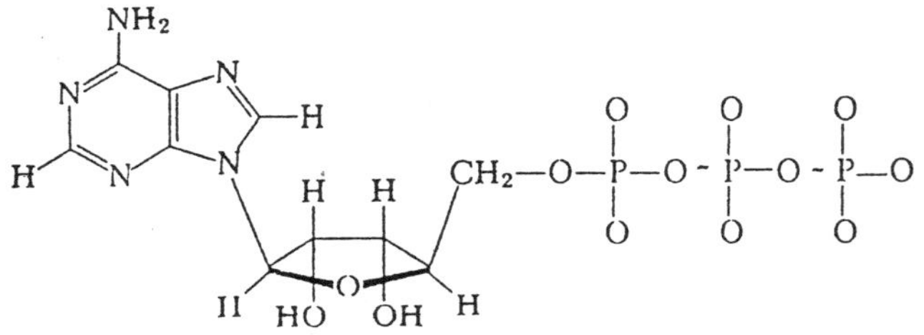

FIGURE 3: ADENOSINE TRIPHOSPHATE

Plants derive ATP from light energy when they produce and store excess carbohydrates, mostly as starch. Through the food chain, the stored energy of plants becomes the potential energy of animals and man. Animals and man, in turn, through their metabolic processes, convert stored plant energy into a usable form of ATP to sustain their life processes. Most of the energy consumed as food is used up as heat, released either directly in the body's metabolic reactions or as a by-product of work performed by the body. Only that part of food energy which is captured in chemical form in the high-energy bonds of ATP can support these functions.

The spiritual act of eating: releasing of the sparks

> ...Man does not live by bread alone, but by all that comes out of God's mouth [*Devarim* 8:3].

The separation of nutrients from waste in the act of eating has its spiritual counterpart in the extraction of the sparks of holiness which are contained in food. And is not the physical and spiritual separation of good from evil the very meaning of human existence?

When a person eats properly, with the right intention, the sparks of holiness from his food attach to his soul, and the waste is forced away [*Yesod v'Shoresh ha-Avodah, sha'ar* 7, ch. 1].

The taste and pleasure that one experiences from food are actually not physical but are derived from the sparks of holiness contained in the food. Not all foods contain an equal amount of sparks and therefore [different foods] are not equal in taste. In general, the less tasty plants contain fewer sparks of holiness, the more tasty plants contain more sparks, and the even tastier animal foods contain the most sparks of holiness. The main energy that a person receives from his food comes from the sparks of holiness contained in the food, which attach themselves to his soul after eating [*Yesod v'Shoresh ha-Avodah, sha'ar* 7, ch. 2].

Blessings and intention

A Jew does not gain true benefit from food without first blessing his Creator. After eating, he further blesses God for sustaining him.

We have already discussed the danger of forgetting God when we are satisfied. God has commanded medicine to be taken for this malady precisely at the dangerous moment when we are the most satisfied — to remember Him through the blessings after food [Rabbenu Bachya, *Shulchan shel Arba'ah*].

When you have eaten and become satisfied, then you must bless the Lord your God for the good land which He has given you [*Devarim* 8:10].

In this world, God's vitalizing force can only come to us clothed in the garment of food....In blessing his food a person shows his recognition of God's vitalizing force and his belief that God's Word is the essential element hidden within the food that he is now eating [*Peri Tzaddik*, "*Es ha-Ochel*"].

While eating, if one recognizes that God has created and

enlivened his food, has provided him with food, and furthermore has added taste to its beneficial elements — taste which arouses desire to increase strength and vitality — then even the pleasure he experiences from eating is purified and sanctified as a sacrifice of the altar [*Peri Tzaddik*, "*Es ha-Ochel*"].

Another aspect of eating is the importance of learning Torah at the table, as our Sages have repeatedly emphasized.

> Rabbi Shimon said, "If three ate at the same table and did not utter words of Torah, it is as if they had partaken of an idolatrous meal" [*Pirkei Avos* 3:3].

Eating in Jewish law and tradition

Discussions on eating in Jewish law are found in tractate *Berachos* of the Talmud and in the *Orach Chayim* section of the *Shulchan Aruch*. Details on permitted and forbidden foods are found in the *Yoreh De'ah* section of the *Shulchan Aruch*. Agricultural restrictions on hybridization, in the sabbatical year, and in the first three years after the planting of fruit trees are found respectively in the tractates *Kilayim*, *Shevi'is*, and *Orlah*. Food preparation on Shabbos is discussed in tractate *Shabbos*; on festivals, in tractate *Beitzah*; and on Pesach, in tractate *Pesachim*. In addition, in the *Abridged Shulchan Aruch*, ch. 32, there is a concise review of proper eating and health. The Rambam is the main source of discussion on health and eating in Jewish law (see his *Mishneh Torah*, *Hilchos De'os*, ch. 4).

The effects of eating

Eating is one of our most common activities. It must be God's Will that we are so involved in eating. There must be an important spiritual purpose to it. If we really can separate good from evil by eating correctly, then this purification has great ramifications upon all levels of reality.

> God made this world one of choice and free will so that we should choose good and abhor evil. Therefore,

sparks of holiness fell into this world, and good and evil were mixed. Man's main service to God is to gather the dispersed sparks of his soul and to raise them up to the level from which the soul has been quarried [*Mor v'Shemesh* on *Parashas Pinchas*].

Moreover, even one's special craving for or aversion to a particular food can be seen as a special sign that God has brought him food that needs rectification [*Shulchan ha-Tahor*, "*Atsmus ha-Achilah*," ch. 6].

When one eats, the holy sparks [of the food] cleave to his soul. By blessing with the right intention before eating and by eating for the sake of Heaven, righteous people purify and raise up the sparks of holiness contained in the food they eat. When a person learns Torah, prays to God, or uses the strength obtained from food to perform a commandment, he elevates the sparks of holiness to the sanctified worlds of Heaven, whence they had originally fallen. The sparks of holiness are thereby returned to their source [*Yesod v'Shoresh ha-Avodah, sha'ar* 7, chs. 1-2].

Releasing sparks and raising up souls

The fallen sparks — or, as they are referred to in various sources, "fallen souls" — return and ascend through the four foundations of inorganic matter, plant matter, animal matter, and human matter. They are raised up from an inorganic to an organic level when plants grow up from the soil, watered by the rain. They are raised up further when the plants in which they are contained are eaten by animals or humans. Likewise, animals are elevated when eaten by humans with proper intention (*Yesod v'Shoresh ha-Avodah, sha'ar* 7, ch. 1).

Atonement of sins — holiness

> Rabbi Yochanan and Rabbi Elazar said, "As long as the Temple stood, the sacrificial altar atoned for Israel; now a man's table atones for him" [*Berachos* 55a].

In other words, the table, upon which we eat, is now our sacrificial altar; our food is our sacrifice; and we, through eating, offer the sacrifice in place of the Temple priest (*Kol Menachem*). Our bodies metabolize this food and thereby release the nutrients and the sparks.

During the times of our Temple in Jerusalem, a chief effect of sacrificing was the elevation and purification of the sparks of holiness contained in the sacrifices. Now that we no longer have the Temple service, our prayers and our eating must serve this function (*Yesod v'Shoresh ha-Avodah, sha'ar* 7, ch. 1).

Our eating for this elevated purpose — for the sake of Heaven — can bring us to holiness and cleaving to God (*Reshis Chachmah, Sha'ar ha-Kedushah* 3:2).

> And it will come to pass, if you diligently obey My commandments which I command you this day, to love the Lord your God and to serve Him with all your heart and with all your soul, then I will give rain for your land at the due time, the early rain and the late rain, and you will gather in your grain, your wine, and your oil. And I will give you grass in your fields for your cattle, so that you can eat and be satisfied [*Devarim* 11:13-15].

The rain falls from above and helps the earth send forth vegetation. Animals feed on the plants and other animals; and, by serving God, man raises mineral, vegetable, and animal matter up to its source. When all the sparks of holiness are raised and returned to their source in Heaven, the way will be prepared for the *Mashiach* to come, we believe soon in our days.

2 | Tu b'Shevat: festival of the trees

> ...Then all the trees of the forest will sing for joy.
> *Tehillim* 96:12

Tu b'Shevat and the renewal of life

Tu b'Shevat, the fifteenth day of the Hebrew month of Shevat, marks the yearly beginning of the regrowth of the fruit of trees. This special day, known as the New Year of the Trees, signifies the time that most of the rainy season has passed in the Land of Israel, the time when the sap begins to rise in the tree trunks and the fruit trees begin to bud (Rashi, *Rosh Hashanah* 14a). We annually witness this welcoming of spring while still in the midst of winter.

Because of the holiness of the Land of Israel and its centrality to the Jews, the seasonal changes there determine when this renewal of life is celebrated. As Jews throughout the world eat fruits on Tu b'Shevat to commemorate the New Year of the Trees in the Land of Israel, we think about the importance of our homeland. Also, we are motivated to study the religious agricultural laws that apply to Eretz Yisrael, such as *shemittah*, *orlah*, *terumah* and *ma'aser*.

The New Year of the Trees is a time to meditate on the wonders of Creation, which are revealed to us through the renewal of life. Tu b'Shevat is a day that should stimulate us to recognize God's miracles which abound in His world and to appreciate God's great kindness, as we witness new life being put into His creation each spring.

The halachic origins of Tu b'Shevat

The exact date of the festival is a subject of controversy in the Talmud, *Beis Shammai* insisting on the first day of Shevat while *Beis Hillel* advocates the fifteenth day of the month (*Rosh Hashanah*, 2a). The ruling of *Beis Hillel* is now accepted.

It has become customary among Jews to celebrate the New Year of the Trees by eating fruits. This practice apparently originated in the Ashkenazic tradition as is cited in the *Shulchan Aruch* (the *Code of Jewish Law*). The commentary Magen Avraham says: "The Ashkenazic Jews have the custom of eating many types of fruit" on the fifteenth of Shevat (*Magen Avraham* 16 on *Shulchan Aruch, Orach Chayim* 131). The source referred to is the *Tikkun Yissachar* (62:25), written by Yissachar Sussan, who was one of the great Sephardic rabbis of Tzefas during the time of Rabbi Yosef Karo, author of the *Shulchan Aruch*, and the great kabbalist Rabbi Yitzchak Luria, known as the Ari Ha-kadosh.

Traditional Sephardic Jews have developed an elaborate fruit ceremony which includes eating thirty fruits. This *Seder Tu b'Shevat* is accompanied by extensive words of Torah, to commemorate the holiday (*Peri Etz Hadar*).

A popular Tu b'Shevat custom is to ask God to bless us with a kosher *esrog* during the following fall's Succos festival.

For man is a tree of the field

> When thou shalt besiege a city a long time, in making war against it to take it, thou shalt not destroy its trees by forcing an axe against them; for thou may eat of them, and thou shalt not cut them down; for is the tree of the field a man, that it should be besieged by thee? [*Devarim*, 20:19]

In many ways man and trees are related, and frequently are interdependent. We often rely on their fruit for food. We use their wood for shelter and various other needs. Their leaves provide us with shade and comfort. Trees, likewise, are affected by our actions, sometimes in an obvious manner and sometimes in a more subtle way.

> From the day that the Temple was destroyed the taste of the fruits has been removed. Rav Yossi says that even the fat of the fruit has been removed [*Sotah* 48a].

> Fruit and grain rot only because of the ways of man [*Tanna d'Vei Eliyahu, Zuta* 3].

There are many similarities between men and trees. Both live off the earth. Trees send down roots to draw sustenance from the soil. Likewise, our food has its origin in the soil that supports the growth of the plants we eat. The animals we eat are themselves nourished from the soil's vegetation. We both take in air, water, and nutrients which are essential to our survival, and both thrive in sunlight. We both produce fruit containing the seeds of the upcoming generations.

Man's body and the tree's trunk are, respectively, their main structural components. Our skin and their bark protect each from harm by outside invaders. Our garments and their leaves protect each and give us our characteristic appearances.

We can learn from trees and their fruit many wonderful insights that can deepen our service to God. David, king of Israel, inspires us and opens our hearts with psalms that often draw a parallel between man and tree:

> And he shall be like a tree planted by streams of water, that brings forth its fruit in its season; its leaf also shall not wither; and in whatever he does he shall prosper [*Tehillim* 1:3].

> The righteous man flourishes like the palm tree; he grows like a cedar in the Lebanon. Those that are planted in the house of the Lord shall flourish in the courts of our God. They still bring forth fruit in old age... [*Tehillim* 92:13-15].

In the fruit garden

As do many discussions on the spiritual effects of eating, ours too returns — for perspective — to the primeval setting of the Garden of Eden and the Tree of Knowledge.

In the beginning, Adam was nourished solely by the fruits of the trees. The Garden of Eden was a luscious fruit garden that provided all of man's physical and spiritual needs. The fragrant garden was filled with trees, all blossoming with rich fruit. In the center of the garden were the two special trees, the Tree of Life and the Tree of Knowledge. These were surrounded by all the other fruit-bearing trees.

These precious, all-nourishing fruits were reserved for humans only, whereas the animals ate simple grasses and field herbs. (*Peri Tzaddik, Tu b'Shevat*)

God created man in such a manner that he must eat to live, and his nourishment was originally taken in holiness, according to God's instructions. In the beginning, God's sole positive commandment to man involved eating the fruit of the Garden of Eden.

> And the Lord God commanded man, saying: "From all the trees of the garden you may surely eat" [*Bereshis* 2:16].

Similarly, the sole negative commandment was the prohibition against eating forbidden fruit.

> "And from the Tree of Knowledge of good and evil you should not eat, since on the day you eat from it you will surely die" [*Bereshis* 2:17].

Man lived in a paradise surrounded by fruit trees; and his subsistence from these trees was effortless. The trees brought forth their fruits, and even fully-prepared cakes, all for man's delight and sustenance. However, darkness descended when the first couple in the world committed the first sin by eating of the forbidden fruit of the Tree of Knowledge of good and evil, as a result of the seductive words of the serpent. This act caused a combination of good and evil throughout the world; it caused many changes in what and how man eats; and it even caused changes in the trees themselves. Many trees ceased to bear fruit completely. In the other trees, most of the nourishing components or nutrients left the fruit, forcing man to expand his food sources in order to receive adequate nourishment. From the time of Adam and Chavah's sin of eating from the Tree of Knowledge, there has been a need for spiritual rectification of food through eating. The act of eating in a holy way, by reciting the proper blessings, by eating kosher food, and by intending to use the energy obtained from the food eaten to serve God, physically and spiritually separates the good from the evil in the food. On the other hand, all the unrighteous behavior on the part of man throughout the generations has had a continuous degrading effect on the quality of the world's fruits (*Chesed l'Avraham* 19).

Rabbi Yehoshua ben Levi explains in the Talmud (*Pesachim* 118a) that after Adam sinned by eating from the Tree of Knowledge, God told him that thereafter he would eat from the herbs of the field. Adam's eyes filled with tears as he asked: "Master of the universe, my donkey and I will eat from the same feed bag?" as previously herbs were eaten by animals and not by man. God then answered sternly: "By the sweat of your brow you will eat bread...." Unlike the grazing and foraging animals, man was destined to work hard for his living and would have to prepare his own food. From that day on the fruits, as well, were cursed and lost their position as the sole sustainers of human life.

Antioxidants — a hint of days of glory

Having forfeited their role as the only source of nutrition for mankind — as reflected by the fact that their present nutritional composition is relatively minor — nevertheless, we do find in fruits small amounts of certain important chemicals, which hint at their glorious past and promising future.

Natural phytochemicals, known as antioxidants, are powerful anti-cancer preventers found commonly in fruits. These protective factors help the plants themselves fight invading infections which threaten their very existence. By eating fruit one's chances of developing cancer may be decreased. Researchers and nutritionists today have evidence that these same substances can fight cancerous cells in humans, as well. Likewise, antioxidants are thought to have a role in the prevention of heart disease.

Nutrition in the end of days

In the Land of Israel every seven years the land is proclaimed "sanctified to God." The Torah forbids us to work our fields for profit, and instructs us to abandon our crops. The seventh or sabbatical year, known as *shemittah*, teaches us to have faith in God in that He will supply our needs, even at this time when we do not work the land. We learn to see God's hand in Creation, and we look forward to the Final Redemption, when God's complete control over His beautiful world will be revealed.

The month of Shevat, like the *shemittah* year, reminds us of God's Creation of the world and of the Final Redemption, as the dry, withered trees of winter begin to show new life and vitality. The month of Shevat heralds the approach of Purim and of Pesach, holidays of joy and redemption. Shevat also is a time for the rectification of improper eating, preparatory to the Purim holiday meal and the eating of matzah and bitter herbs on Pesach (*Peri Tzaddik,Tu b'Shevat* 35). According to *Beis Shammai*, this spiritual work begins on the very first day of the month of Shevat.

The special day of Tu b'Shevat reminds us of the importance of rectifying the sin of eating from the Tree of Knowledge. By this rectification we hasten the ultimate Redemption. We recite the blessing over fruit before eating, to add to its holiness. We hope that proper eating on our part will affect the fruit trees as well as ourselves, restoring us to the position we once held in the Garden of Eden (*Bereshis Rabbah* 12). As we eat the fruits of Tu b'Shevat, our soul yearns to reach the level of eating enjoyed by Adam before he sinned, when he ate only from the trees of the garden and was totally nourished by these holy fruits.

The Talmud relates the story of Rabbi Shimon bar Yochai, who fled from Roman persecution at the time of the destruction of the Second Temple and hid with his son in a cave in the mountains (*Shabbos* 33b). Their sole source of food was the nearby carob tree, which sustained them for many years until they came out of hiding. This story reminds us of the special all-nourishing trees of the Garden of Eden. Perhaps it also hints at a future time when once again trees alone will be able to sustain human life.

In the World-to-Come, when the *Mashiach* has arrived, trees will regain the complete strength that they possessed in the Garden of Eden before the sin. The non-fruit-bearing trees will all begin to bear fruit! As the Talmud states:

> Rabbi Chiya ben Ashi said in the name of Rav: "In future days, the non-fruit-bearing trees of Israel will be loaded down with fruits..." [*Kesubbos* 112b].

Then the trees will all sing God's praise (*Perek Shirah* 3), as King David predicted:

> ...Then all the trees of the forest will sing for joy [*Tehillim* 96:12].

All fruits will increase in size, taste, and beauty, especially those in the Land of Israel (*Chesed l'Avraham* 19). According to Rabban Gamliel, these future trees will bear new fruit daily. The trees of the Land of Israel will also produce fully-formed cakes, as they did at the beginning of Creation (*Shabbos* 30b), and there will be no lack of food.

The Midrash adds that in the World-to-Come man will be ultimately healed by eating the fruits of the Garden of Eden (*Devarim Rabbah* 1:1 and *Shemos Rabbah* 15:21).

May it be God's Will that we should reach that destination where the trees will sing God's praise and nourish us and heal us completely.

3 | The apple: symbol of health

You have entered the orchard of the tree of the holy apples. The sight of the beautiful, lush apple tree with its sweet-smelling fruit overwhelms you. It is a sight and fragrance that you have never before experienced. You stand in the Garden of Eden and gaze in amazement at your surroundings. In the background are many other fruit-bearing trees of various kinds. What is the inner meaning of the beautiful apple tree and its fruit? You are overwhelmed by a desire to know the full meaning of all that you are experiencing. It is clear that the apple tree and its fruit are not simple phenomena; nor are the other trees. They represent the essence of life on its deepest level.

The apple tree: symbol of Hashem

The Gemara, in *Ta'anis* 5b, compares Hashem to a fruit tree. A tired, hungry and thirsty traveler passing through a desert, comes upon a tree whose fruit is sweet, whose shade is pleasant, and at whose base flows a stream. The traveler eats from the fruit, drinks from the water, and rests in the shade of the tree. When he rises to leave, he proclaims: "Tree, tree, how can I bless you? If I would say that you should have sweet fruit, you already have it; that your shade should be pleasant, it already is; that a stream of water should pass by you, you already have a passing stream. Therefore, may it be His Will that all your offspring should be as yourself."

In this parable, the stream represents the Torah, from which

The apple: symbol of health

all those who thirst for the word of God may drink. The fruit is the children — the Jewish people — who, we pray, will grow in holiness, following the ways of the tree. And the tree clearly represents Hashem, may His Name be blessed, Who is the paragon of perfection (Vilna Gaon, *Shir ha-Shirim* 2:3).

We read in *Shir ha-Shirim* (2:3):

> Like the apple tree among the trees of the forest, so is my Beloved among the sons. I sat down under His shadow with great delight, and His fruit was sweet to my taste.

Rashi explains that the apple tree represents Hashem, our God, Who is distinguished from the false gods.

In *Perek Shirah* (3:27), similarly, we learn:

> The apple says (*Shir ha-Shirim* 2:3): "Like the apple tree among the trees of the forest, so is my Beloved among the sons."

The apple tree blossoms in the spring, in the month of Nisan, and its fruit ripens fifty days later, in the month of Sivan. This is likened to Hashem's giving of the Torah: He redeemed us from Egypt in Nisan, and after fifty days gave us His Torah (*Shir ha-Shirim Rabbah* 2). Having received the Torah, the Jewish People now sit, figuratively speaking, in the shade of Hashem, protected by Him and by His Torah.

The holy *Zohar*, as well, often praises Hashem through the symbol of the apple:

> The apple is distinguished in color from all the trees [*Zohar, Ha'azinu*].
>
> The apple's taste is sweet [*ibid., Acharei Mos*].
>
> The apple has a finer fragrance than all the other trees [*ibid.*].
>
> The apple heals all [*ibid.*].

All these references to apple mean Hashem, Who is most exalted in His appearance, taste, fragrance, and healing ability.

Rabbi Tzaddok Ha-kohen (*Peri Tzaddik, Shelach* 52) explains that the Tree of Life refers to the Holy One, blessed be He, Who is called "the apple tree." This, again, refers to the *pasuk*, "Like the apple tree among the trees of the forest...."

The tree, of course, is merely a symbol. Our limited minds obviously cannot comprehend the Infinite One. The apples of the tree are just representations of a spiritual phenomenon. The Torah speaks in terms that human minds can comprehend; it uses a physical sign to point to a spiritual reality. We are really talking about a spiritual tree giving rise to spiritual apples.

The main revelation of Godliness and of the flow of life-giving vitality from Heaven is provided through the symbol of the Tree of Life, which also represents the Torah, and from there the vitality spreads to all the trees of the Garden of Eden, and on and on, to the entire Creation.

The sweet apple: symbol of the Jewish people

...and its fruit was sweet to my taste [*Shir ha-Shirim* 2:3].

The fruits of this special tree (which symbolizes Hashem) are its offspring, the Jewish people, who are commanded by Hashem to grow in the way of holiness, following the example of Hashem and His holy Torah. Rabbi Tzaddok Ha-kohen explains that the fruits of the Tree of Life represent the souls of the righteous, which are like sweet fruit to God's palate (*Peri Tzaddik, Shelach* 52).

We recall that when Ya'akov *Avinu* came to his father, Yitzchak, to receive his blessing, Yitzchak sensed the aroma of Ya'akov's clothes and remarked, "My son's fragrance is like the fragrance of the field which is blessed by Hashem" (*Bereshis* 27:27). Rashi explains here that the sweet fragrance was that of the Garden of Eden, which entered with Ya'akov; the fragrance of the field blessed by Hashem is the fragrance of the field of the holy apples.

In kabbalistic writings, the Friday night Shabbos meal also is referred to as "the field of the holy apples." That is the time when the *Shechinah*, Hashem's Divine Presence, dwells among the Jewish People, when we receive the holiness of the entering Shabbos Queen (*Peri Tzaddik, Shemini Atzeres*). It is at that special time that the Jewish People are called "holy apples"

(*Peri Tzaddik, Shelach* 53).

The Ben Ish Chai also connects the apple to the field of the holy apples and the *pasuk* "My son's fragrance is like the fragrance of the field...." He explains, further, that this is why we eat apples during the evening meals on Rosh Hashanah, since the apple is distinguished in three ways — taste, appearance, and fragrance — as we have mentioned previously (*Halachos, Nitzavim*). We eat apples as a sign that we will be blessed with children, life, and sustenance throughout the new year (*Shulchan Aruch, Orach Chayim* 3, *Hilchos Rosh Hashanah*, Taz).

The Gemara (*Shabbos* 88a) compares the Jewish People to the apple with regard to our receiving the Torah at Mt. Sinai. Just as the blossoming of the apple tree precedes the formation of leaves, so the Jewish People agreed to perform the Torah's commandments even before hearing them (*Na'aseh v'nishma*). Rashi explains (*Shabbos* 88a) that in most trees the leaves grow before the fruit blossoms. Apple trees, however, blossom before they develop leaves. This process, specific to the apple tree, illustrates the unusual character of the Jewish People, who are ready to perform Hashem's Will unconditionally.

The apple, ultimately, symbolizes our connection to Hashem. We are likened to the apple just as Hashem is compared to the apple tree. Hashem expects us to live in holiness, just as He is holy. The Midrash (*Tanchuma, Kedoshim*) presents the example of a king who married. The king explains to his new bride: "Since you married me and I am the king, you are therefore the queen; just as I am 'Your Royal Highness,' so you are 'Your Highness.'" Likewise, just as Hashem is the King, so we, the Jewish People, are His queen, by association. In the same manner, the apples, i.e., the Jewish People, are attached to the apple tree, Hashem.

Nutritional aspects of the apple

Just as we, the Jewish People, are not on the spiritual level of our ancestors, so the apple, to which we are likened, is not on a nutritional par with apples of the past. All fruits, the apple included, have decreased in nutritional value since Adam and Chavah's sin of eating the fruit of the Tree of Knowledge (*Chesed l'Avraham* 19). The decline continued; and, as the Gemara explains (*Sotah* 48a), after the destruction of the Temple the fruits declined even more rapidly. The apple is now practically devoid of major nutrients, as the accompanying chart indicates.

APPLE — raw, unpeeled 4.6 ounces (138 g.)			
NUTRIENT	AMOUNT	U.S. RDA	
		MEN (25-50 years)	WOMEN (25-50 years)
calcium	10 mg.	800 mg.	800 mg.
calories	81	2900	2200
carbohydrate	21 g.	363 g.	275 g.
copper	0.05 mg.	2.3 mg.	2.3 mg.
fat	0.49 g.	96.7 g.	73.3 g.
fiber	1.1 g.	(no RDA)	(no RDA)
folacin	3.9 mcg.	200 mcg.	180 mcg.
iron	0.25 mg.	10 mg.	15 mg.
magnesium	6 mg.	350 mg.	280 mg.
manganese	0.06 mg.	3.5 mg.	3.5 mg.
niacin	0.11 mg.	19 mg.	15 mg.
phosphorus	10 mg.	800 mg.	800 mg.
potassium	159 mg.	2000 mg.	2000 mg.
protein	0.27 g.	63 g.	50 g.
riboflavin	0.02 mg.	1.7 mg.	1.3 mg.
thiamin	0.02 mg.	1.5 mg.	1.1 mg.
vitamin A	74 IU	3333 IU	2667 IU
vitamin B_6	0.01 mg.	2 mg.	1.6 mg.
vitamin B_{12}	0	2 mcg.	2 mcg.
vitamin C	7.3 mg.	60 mg.	60 mg.
zinc	0.05 mg.	15 mg.	12 mg.

Despite its dismal nutritional appearance, the apple does contain various healing agents which are not apparent when one uses standard procedures of assessing nutritional composition. These healing agents relate to both of today's greatest health problems: heart disease and cancer. The apple contains agents that can lower blood cholesterol levels, a major risk factor in heart disease, as well as cancer-preventing agents.

Antioxidants — phytochemicals present in apples in very small amounts — are powerful cancer and heart-disease preventers. Flavonoids are polyphenolic antioxidants that occur naturally in vegetables and fruits, and apples are a major source of flavonoids. Flavonoids help to lower blood cholesterol levels and prevent blood clotting, thus reducing the likelihood of a fatal heart attack. Flavonoid intake has been shown to have an inverse correlation with mortality from coronary heart disease (*Lancet*, vol. 342 [October 23, 1993], pp. 1007-1011).

Apples also contain nutritional fiber, which has a protective influence on our health. Nutritionists generally speak of two types of fiber, soluble and insoluble. Soluble fibers are non-nutrient components that are soluble in water; insoluble fibers are not water-soluble. The apple, fortunately, contains both types of fiber, with all of their disease-preventing benefits.

The soluble fibers have the potential to lower serum lipid (fat, i.e., cholesterol, triglyceride) levels. Pectin, a major soluble fiber, is present in significant amounts in apples. Apples are the most common food source for cholesterol-lowering pectin.

The apple peel, which mainly consists of insoluble or undigestible fiber, has long been noted for its anti-constipation and anti-cancer potential.

Every apple, then, has the potential to contribute to our health!

"Heal us, Hashem"

In *Shir ha-Shirim* (2:5) King Solomon writes: "Invigorate me with apples." The apple, in our time as well, symbolizes good health, as reflected in the popular folk saying, "An apple a day keeps the doctor away!"

The Zohar speaks of the apple's healing quality:

> Just as the apple heals all, so the Holy One, blessed be He, heals all [*Zohar, Acharei Mos*].

The Zohar continues:

> Just as the apple has various colors (white, red, green), so the Holy One, blessed be He, has various supernal colors (white, red, and green, corresponding to the attributes of *chesed, gevurah,* and *tiferes*) [*Zohar, Acharei Mos; Ziv ha-Zohar, Va'eschanan*].

The symbol of the green apple reveals some of the hidden meaning behind the Zohar's teaching. *Tiferes*, the kabbalistic attribute of mercy and beauty, is associated with the color green, the color of healing. The word *tiferes* derives from the root *pe'er*, as reflected in the word *refuah*, healing.

Ya'akov *Avinu*, has a special connection to health, as the Gemara relates: "Our father Ya'akov did not die" (*Ta'anis* 5b). Ya'akov is the patriarch associated with the attribute of *tiferes* and balance, as he represents the harmony between the aspects of kindness and severity. Likewise, Ya'akov is associated with apples, as Yitzchak sensed a fragrance of apples which entered with Ya'akov when he came for his father's blessing, as explained previously.

The Ben Ish Chai writes that the apple tree is the only fruit tree that has its spiritual source in the attribute of *tiferes*. This is yet another indication of the apple's special connection to healing (*Halachos, Nitzavim*).

Our ultimate goal is to connect ourselves, like apples, to the tree, Hashem. We can do this only by learning and living by Hashem's commandments, totally for the sake of Heaven. Spiritual health is the source of physical health. Torah is the remedy. Spiritual perfection — full Torah observance — is the gateway to physical health.

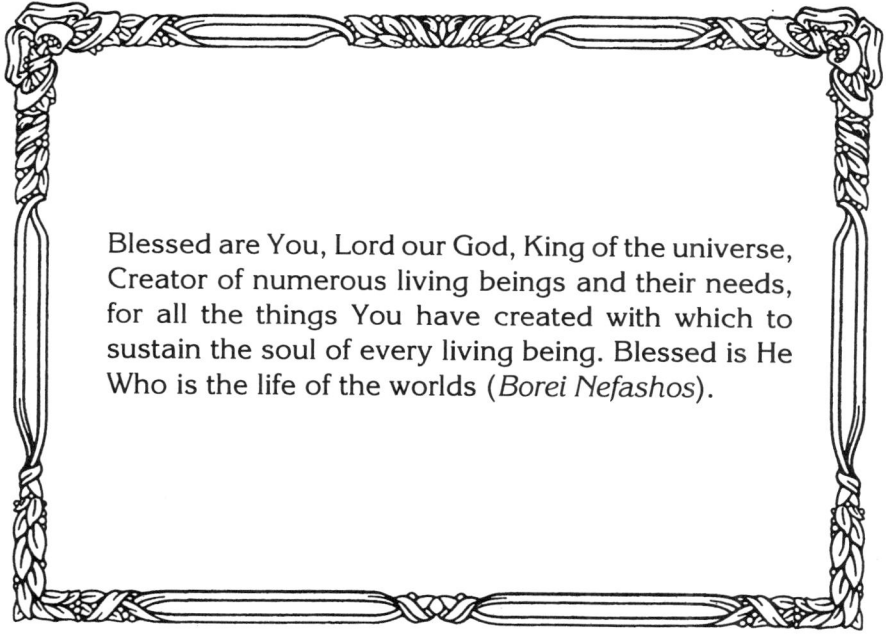

Blessed are You, Lord our God, King of the universe, Creator of numerous living beings and their needs, for all the things You have created with which to sustain the soul of every living being. Blessed is He Who is the life of the worlds (*Borei Nefashos*).

Appendices

APPENDIX 1 | About calories

What is a calorie?

A calorie is the unit of measurement that tells you how much energy you get from the foods you eat. Different foods provide different amounts of energy. To control your weight you will need to control the amount of energy (the number of calories) you get from food, and the amount of energy you use up in exercise and normal activity. If your food provides more calories than you use, you gain weight. If it gives fewer, you lose. If it provides just enough, your weight should remain about the same.

For every 3,500 extra calories you get and do not use, you gain about one pound (half a kilogram), which is stored food energy in the form of fat. To lose excess fat you must use up stored energy by:

1. eating less food (fewer calories), forcing your body to draw energy from its stored fat;

2. increasing your activity, to use up more energy; or

3. doing both: eating less and exercising more.

Caloric needs

Guide your food intake in relation to your caloric needs. These depend on your sex, size, physical activity, and age. As a general guide, we have listed daily caloric recommendations for

About calories

people of medium size and activity.

Calories Needed Per Day

Age	Male	Female
11-14	2,800	2,400
15-18	3,000	2,100
22-44	3,000	2,100
45-64	2,700	2,000
65+	2,400	1,800

Everyone, even a person trying to lose weight, should generally consume at least 1,200 calories per day, unless otherwise instructed by his nutritionist or dietitian.

CALORIE TABLES

For your convenience, foods are listed below in the following groups: beverages; breads and cereals; dairy foods; desserts and snacks; fats and oils, nuts and seeds; fruits and juices; fish, poultry, meat, eggs, and legumes; and vegetables.

As a general rule each day, you should choose two servings from the dairy group, two servings from the fish, etc. group, four servings altogether from the fruits and the vegetables, and four servings from the breads and cereals. Select nutrients carefully for health and for weight control.

Beverages*

ALCOHOLIC BEVERAGES	Quantity	Calories
beer	12 oz. (360 cc.)	146
vodka, 80 proof	1.5 oz. (45 cc.)	97
whiskey, 86 proof	1.5 oz. (45 cc.)	105
wine	3.5 oz. (105 cc.)	74

		Calories
CARBONATED BEVERAGES		
cola	12 oz. (360 cc.)	151
lemon-lime soda	12 oz. (360 cc.)	149
orange soda	12 oz. (360 cc.)	177
OTHER		
coffee, instant	1 tsp.	4
tea	6 oz. (180 cc.)	2
tea, herbal	6 oz. (180 cc.)	1
water		0

*Not including milk and fruit juices.

Breads and cereals

Enriched and whole-grain breads and cereals are important sources of vitamins B_1, B_2, niacin, and iron.

	Quantity	Calories
BREADS		
cracked-wheat	1 slice	66
French	1 slice	81
matzah	1	80
pita	1/2	106
rye	1 slice	66
white	1 slice	64
whole-wheat	1 slice	61
CRACKERS		
rice cake	1	35
soda cracker	2	35
MUFFINS		
bran	1	112
corn	1	115
plain	1	135

About calories

ROLLS   *Calories*

plain, pan	1	85
whole-wheat	1	72

GRAIN PRODUCTS

macaroni	1 cup	159
rice	1 cup	180
spaghetti	1 cup	159
wheat germ	1/4 cup (1 oz., 30 g.)	108

CEREALS

bran flakes	3/4 cup	93
corn flakes	1 1/4 cup	110
cream of rice	3/4 cup	95
granola	1/4 cup	123
oatmeal, cooked	2/3 cup	108
popcorn, no oil	1 cup	23
popcorn, with oil	1 cup	40
puffed rice	1 cup	57
puffed wheat	1 cup	52
rice krispies	1 cup	112

Dairy foods

Dairy products are important sources of calcium, protein, and vitamins A, B_2, B_6 and B_{12}.

	Quantity	*Calories*
cheese, American	3 oz. (90 g.)	318
cheese, cottage, 1% fat	3 oz. (90 g.)	68
	1 cup	164
cheese, cottage, 4% fat	1 cup	239
cheese, white, no fat	3 oz. (90 g.)	69
cheese, white, 5% fat	3 oz. (90 g.)	132
milk, chocolate, 1% fat	1 cup (240 cc.)	158
milk, chocolate, 4% fat	1 cup (240 cc.)	208
milk, goat	1 cup (240 cc.)	168

		Calories
milk, 1% fat	1 cup (240 cc.)	102
milk, skim	1 cup (240 cc.)	86
milk, 4% fat	1 cup (240 cc.)	150
yogurt, plain	1 cup (240 cc.)	139
yogurt, skim	1 cup (240 cc.)	127

Desserts and snacks

	Quantity	Calories
butter cookies	10	229
cake, cheese	1 piece	257
cake, chocolate	1 slice (2 oz.)	220
cake, white	1 slice (2 oz.)	211
chocolate bar, bittersweet	1 oz. (30 g.)	135
chocolate bar, milk	1 oz. (30 g.)	150
chocolate syrup	2 tbsp.	92
cinnamon roll	1	110
Danish pastry	1	161
hard candy	1 oz. (30 g.)	109
honey	1 tbsp.	64
ice cream, chocolate	1/2 cup	280
vanilla	1/2 cup	135
ice cream bar, with chocolate coating	1	330
jello	1/2 cup	81
jelly	1 tbsp.	49
pretzels	5 small sticks	20
pudding	1/2 cup	181
sandwich cookies	4	198
sugar	1 tsp.	15
tea biscuits	6	130
waffle cremes	3	150

Fats and oils, nuts and seeds

Fats and oils are important sources of vitamin E and essential fatty acids. They are high-calorie foods.

About calories

	Quantity	Calories
almonds	24 (1 oz., 30 g.)	167
butter	1 tbsp.	108
cashews	1 oz. (30 g.)	163
chestnuts	1 oz. (30 g.)	70
coconut, dried	1 oz. (30 g.)	187
margarine	1 tbsp.	100
mayonnaise	1 tbsp.	99
oil, olive	1 tbsp.	119
oil, soybean	1 tbsp.	120
oil, sunflower	1 tbsp.	120
peanuts, dry roasted	1 oz. (30 g.)	164
pecans	1 oz. (30 g.)	187
pistachio nuts	1 oz. (30 g.)	172
pumpkin seeds	1 oz. (30 g.)	148
sesame seeds	1 tbsp.	52
sour cream	1 tbsp.	26
sunflower seeds	1 oz. (30 g.)	165
techina (sesame butter)	1 tbsp.	89
walnuts	1 oz. (30 g.)	172

Fruits and juices

Fruits are important sources of vitamin A, vitamin C, fiber, and potassium.

FRUITS	Quantity	Calories
apple	1 medium	81
applesauce, sweetened	1/2 cup	97
unsweetened	1/2 cup	53
apricots, fresh	3 medium	51
dried	6 halves	50
banana	1 medium	105
cactus	1 medium	35
cherries	10	49
dates, dried	10	228
figs, fresh	1 medium	37
dried	10	477

		Calories
grapefruit	1/2	39
grapes	1 cup	114
guava	1	45
loquat	10	47
mango	1	135
melon, honeydew	1/4 cup (3 oz., 90 g.)	33
orange	1	65
papaya	1	117
peach	1	37
pear	1	98
persimmon	1	32
pineapple	1 cup	77
plum	1	36
pomegranate	1	104
prunes	2	40
raisins	2/3 cup	300
strawberries	1 cup	45
tangerine	1	37
watermelon	1 cup	50

JUICES

apple juice	8 fl. oz. (240 cc.)	116
apricot nectar	8 fl. oz. (240 cc.)	141
grape juice	8 fl. oz. (240 cc.)	155
orange juice	8 fl. oz. (240 cc.)	111
prune juice	4 fl. oz. (120 cc.)	90
tomato juice	8 fl. oz. (240 cc.)	43

Fish, poultry, meat, eggs, and legumes

These foods are important sources of protein, iron, and B-vitamins.

	Quantity	Calories
FISH		
carp	3 oz. (90 g.)	108
gefilte	1 piece	35

About calories

		Calories
halibut	3 oz. (90 g.)	93
herring, pickled	1 oz. (30 g.)	78
raw	1 oz. (30 g.)	45
salmon	3 oz. (90 g.)	99
sardines, in oil	2	50
sole, fillet	3 oz. (90 g.)	60
trout	3 oz. (90 g.)	100
tuna, in oil	2 oz. (60 g.)	170
in water	2 oz. (60 g.)	60

POULTRY

chicken, dark meat, without skin, roasted	3 1/2 oz. (100 g.)	205
chicken, light meat,		
with skin, fried	3 1/2 oz. (100 g.)	246
with skin, roasted	3 1/2 oz. (100 g.)	222
without skin, roasted	3 1/2 oz. (100 g.)	173
turkey, light or dark meat		
with skin, roasted	3 1/2 oz. (100 g.)	208
without skin, roasted	3 1/2 oz. (100 g.)	170

MEAT

chuck, roast	3 1/2 oz. (100 g.)	350
frankfurter, beef	1 (2 oz., 60 g.)	180
ground beef, broiled	3 1/2 oz. (100 g.)	287
lamb chop, broiled	2 oz. (60 g.)	273
liver, beef, pan-fried	3 1/2 oz. (100 g.)	217
salami	1 slice (1 oz., 30 g.)	78

EGGS

boiled	1	79
fried	1	83
white	1	16
yolk	1	63

LEGUMES

		Calories
beans, baked	1 cup	235
chick-peas, boiled	1 cup	269
lentils, boiled	1 cup	231
lima beans, boiled	1 cup	217
peas, split, boiled	1 cup	231
soybeans, boiled	1 cup	298
tofu, raw	1/2 cup	94

Vegetables

Vegetables are important sources of vitamin A and vitamin C, are high in fiber content and, except for avocado, are low in calories.

	Quantity	Calories
avocado	1 medium	306
beets, boiled	1/2 cup	26
broccoli, boiled	1/2 cup	23
cabbage, raw	1/2 cup	8
carrots, raw	1 medium	31
boiled	1/2 cup	35
cauliflower, boiled	1/2 cup	15
celery, raw	1 stalk	6
corn, boiled	1/2 cup	89
cucumber	1/2 cup	7
eggplant, boiled	1/2 cup	13
garlic	3 cloves	13
green beans, boiled	1/2 cup	22
kohlrabi	1/2 cup	24
lettuce, romaine	1/2 cup	4
mushrooms, boiled	1/2 cup	21
olives, green, pickled	10	45
onion, raw	1/2 cup	27
peas, boiled	1/2 cup	67
pepper, green or red, raw	1/2 cup	12
pickle	1 medium	7

About calories

		Calories
potato, boiled, no skin	1 medium	116
fried	10 pieces	111
mashed	1/2 cup	111
pumpkin, boiled	1/2 cup	24
radish	10 small	7
spinach, boiled	1/2 cup	21
squash, boiled	1/2 cup	18
sweet potato, baked	1 medium	118
boiled	1/2 cup	172
tomato, raw	1 medium	24
tomato paste	1/2 cup	110
turnip, boiled	1/2 cup	14

Desirable weights

Compare your present weight with the desirable weight for your height and frame in order to determine whether you need to lose weight and how much you should lose.

Desirable Weights for Men (in pounds)
(age 25 and up)

Height (ft., in.)	Small Frame	Medium Frame	Large Frame
5'1"	112-120	118-129	126-141
5'2"	115-123	121-133	129-144
5'3"	118-126	124-136	132-148
5'4"	121-129	127-139	135-152
5'5"	124-133	130-143	138-156
5'6"	128-137	134-147	142-161
5'7"	132-141	138-152	147-166
5'8"	136-145	142-156	151-170
5'9"	140-150	146-160	155-174
5'10"	144-154	150-165	159-179
5'11"	148-158	154-170	164-184
6'0"	152-162	158-175	168-189
6'1"	156-167	162-180	173-194
6'2"	160-171	167-185	178-199
6'3"	164-175	172-190	182-204

Desirable Weights for Women (in pounds)
(age 25 and up)

Height (ft., in.)	Small Frame	Medium Frame	Large Frame
4'8"	92-98	96-107	104-119
4'9"	94-101	98-110	106-122
4'10"	96-104	101-113	109-125
4'11"	99-107	104-116	112-128
5'0"	102-110	107-119	115-131
5'1"	105-113	110-122	118-134
5'2"	108-116	113-126	121-138
5'3"	111-119	116-130	125-142
5'4"	114-123	120-135	129-146
5'5"	118-127	124-139	133-150
5'6"	122-131	128-143	137-154
5'7"	126-135	132-147	141-158
5'8"	130-140	136-151	145-163
5'9"	134-144	140-155	149-168
5'10"	138-148	144-159	153-173

APPENDIX 2 | Avoiding a heart attack

> **Heart Health Checklist**
>
> Check the risk factors that apply to you:
>
> ❏ OVERWEIGHT
>
> ❏ HIGH CHOLESTEROL LEVEL
>
> ❏ HIGH BLOOD PRESSURE
>
> ❏ CIGARETTE SMOKING
>
> ❏ LACK OF EXERCISE
>
> ❏ DIABETES
>
> ❏ FAMILY HISTORY OF HEART DISEASE
>
> ❏ STRESS

If any of the above items apply to you, it is recommended that you obtain medical care as well as counseling from a certified nutritionist or dietitian (R.D.). A combination of two or more factors greatly multiplies the risk. On the other hand, early reversal of these factors improves one's chances of avoiding a heart attack at an early age. The American Heart Association has called heart disease "the disease of prosperity." The problem is often one of overnutrition — especially regarding certain types of foods — combined with unhealthy living habits.

The eight risk factors

1. OVERWEIGHT

   Aside from the possible effects of overweight on blood pressure, cholesterol level, or diabetes, extra weight by itself adds to the risk of heart disease. Middle-aged men who are 30% overweight are twice as likely to suffer a heart attack as are middle-aged men of normal weight.

2. HIGH CHOLESTEROL LEVEL

   Studies have shown that a man with a blood cholesterol level of 250 mg. or above is about three times as likely to suffer a heart attack as is a man with a cholesterol level below 194. Some sources report an increased risk up to six times greater.

   Meat and dairy foods are high in saturated fat, while eggs and organ meats are high in cholesterol. A diet rich in these foods tends to raise the level of cholesterol in the blood. A high cholesterol level contributes to the development of atherosclerotic plaques that block arteries, which increases the risk of a heart attack.

3. HIGH BLOOD PRESSURE

   A person whose blood pressure at systole (when the heart contracts) is over 150 is more than twice as likely to have a heart attack as is a man with systolic blood pressure under 120. Some studies report that the risk is up to eight times as great.

   Blood pressure is the pressure put on the walls of the arteries as the heart pumps blood through them. Some cases of high blood pressure (hypertension) are caused by disease, which can be diagnosed and treated. However, the cause of the most common kind of hypertension is unknown. Treatment may include dietary changes to bring weight down, drugs to lower the pressure, elimination of cigarette smoking, and modification of stressful living habits. High blood pressure, if untreated, increases the risk of having a heart attack, a stroke, or kidney failure.

4. CIGARETTE SMOKING

A man who smokes more than one pack of cigarettes a day faces almost twice the risk of having a heart attack as does a non-smoker. It has been found that smokers develop coronary disease at a rate that is three to six times greater than that among non-smokers.

It is important to note that the death rate among people who stop smoking is nearly as low as it is among people who never smoked. On the other hand, the earlier a person begins to smoke, the greater the risk to his health in future years.

5. LACK OF EXERCISE

The sedentary man runs twice the risk of the active man. Exercise tones the muscles, stimulates the circulation, and helps to prevent overweight, as well as lowering cholesterol levels in the blood. On the other hand, strenuous and unaccustomed activity occasionally brings on a heart attack in a person who has atherosclerosis of the coronary arteries. Therefore, exercise should be increased gradually when desirable. High-risk persons should exercise only after consulting with their physician.

6. DIABETES

In middle age, diabetes increases the risk of a heart attack by two to four times. When excess sugar builds up in the blood of a diabetic person, it may contribute to the development of atherosclerosis in combination with cholesterol and other fats in the blood. In its mild form as it is usually found during middle age, especially among the overweight, diabetes can escape detection for many years. If it goes untreated too long, it may cause severe disability, and it greatly increases the risks of heart attack and stroke.

7. FAMILY HISTORY OF HEART DISEASE

A tendency to atherosclerosis may run in your family if you had close relatives who died between ages 40 and 60 from the complications of this disease. Even if you have inherited this tendency, the way you live will have a great influence on your chances of developing atherosclerosis and of having a heart attack. The existence of such a family history would emphasize the importance of reducing all other risk factors.

8. STRESS

The role of tension and stress as a risk factor in heart disease is as yet unclear. Both emotion and stress can affect fat and cholesterol levels, at least on a temporary basis. Stress, therefore, combined with other risk factors, appears to increase one's chances of having a heart attack.

Reversal of risk factors so as to avoid heart disease

Most of the evidence today indicates that reducing the known risks will prevent heart attacks. To minimize the risks, one should follow these guidelines:

1. Achieve and/or maintain your ideal weight, but avoid extreme reducing diets.
2. Eat less of high cholesterol foods.
3. Limit fat to 30% of your caloric intake; reduce saturated fats (mostly from animal sources) in your diet to one-third of your total fat intake.
4. Seek treatment for high blood pressure.
5. Stop smoking.
6. Increase exercise gradually.
7. Control diabetes.
8. Reduce stress.

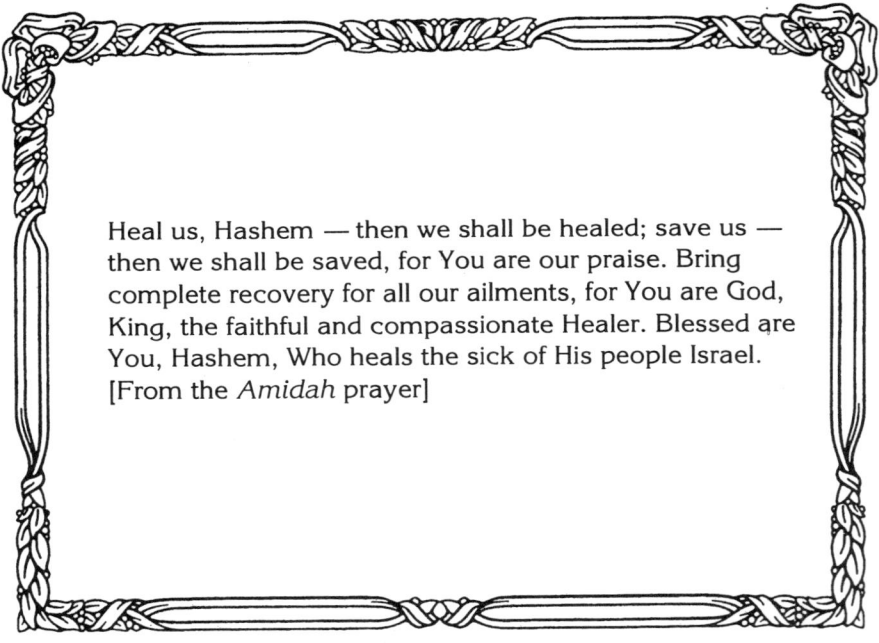

Heal us, Hashem — then we shall be healed; save us — then we shall be saved, for You are our praise. Bring complete recovery for all our ailments, for You are God, King, the faithful and compassionate Healer. Blessed are You, Hashem, Who heals the sick of His people Israel.
[From the *Amidah* prayer]

APPENDIX 3 | What is a nutritionist?

Medicine arose from dietetics. Early physicians (including Hippocrates) used diet to prevent and cure diseases, and used drugs only if a dietary approach failed.

A nutritionist is a medical specialist who promotes good health through modification of food habits. Therapy includes counseling on principles of normal nutrition to maintain good health, as well as manipulation of food intake, and decreasing or increasing nutrients, in the treatment of disease. A skilled nutritionist must combine extensive training in the sciences and social sciences with a caring attitude and sensitivity to his patient's feelings and situation.

The Rambam, over 800 years ago, recommended a three-step approach to medical care:

1. diet only, whenever possible;

2. light medication, if diet alone is not sufficient to treat the disease;

3. strong medication, only when absolutely necessary, and only in the hands of a qualified, experienced physician.

Health problems that can be corrected by diet alone are all that the nutritionist will treat without consulting a physician. Many medical doctors now regularly refer patients requiring nutritional care to a nutritionist.

Treatments do not involve giving the same standard diet to

each patient. After questioning by the nutritionist to obtain a list of the patient's likes and dislikes, the nutritionist and the patient agree on a diet that will be the most comfortable, so as to encourage long-term dietary compliance.

The training and qualifications of a medical nutritionist

An academic background with a degree from a recognized university is the first requirement in order to be a nutritionist. Training includes a series of courses in science, such as biology, chemistry, human physiology, biochemistry, and microbiology. In addition, many courses in normal nutrition and nutrition in disease are required, with in-depth studies of vitamins and nutritional biochemistry.

This training now entails a minimum of four years of full-time study. A second degree in nutrition (M.S.) is given after an additional two years of course work. With successful completion of this study as well as several months of training in a hospital under an experienced nutritionist, the qualified student may then apply for a license to practice.

Persons wishing to contact the author may write or call:
Yaakov Levinson, B.A., M.S.
Director, The Israel Nutrition Institute
27 Hakablan Street
Har Nof, Jerusalem, Israel 93874
Tel. 02-513717

APPENDIX 4 | Sources

Chesed l'Avraham. A kabbalistic work by Rabbi Avraham Azulai, one of the great Torah Sages of Spain who later resided in Chevron.

Chumash (*Bereshis, Devarim,* cited). The five books of the Torah given by God to the Jewish people on Mount Sinai.

Commentary on the Torah by Rabbi Moshe ben Nachman (the Ramban, 1194-1270). One of the leading spiritual leaders of his time, the Ramban headed a yeshiva in Gerona, Spain, and wrote over fifty works on the Torah, the Talmud, Jewish law, philosophy, Kabbalah, and medicine.

Da'as Tevunos. A kabbalistic work by Rabbi Moshe Chayim Luzzatto (the Ramchal, 1701-45), who, following the controversy caused in his native Italy by his kabbalistic writings, moved to Amsterdam, where he wrote his highly acclaimed *Mesillas Yesharim* (*The Path of the Righteous*), a step-by-step program for any Jew to attain moral perfection.

Eliyahu Zuta. See below, *Tanna d'Vei Eliyahu.*

Halachos. A halachic, kabbalistic work by Rabbi Yosef Chaim, the "Ben Ish Chai" of Bagdad.

Hilchos De'os. A chapter of the Rambam's *Mishneh Torah* (see below) which presents the laws and views of the Torah on human behavior.

Kitzur Shulchan Aruch. A widely used, lucid abridgment of the *Shulchan Aruch* (see below), written in Hungary by Rabbi Shelomo Ganzfried (1804-86).

Kol Menachem. A chasidic work by the present Kaliver Rebbe of Bnei Brak.

Magen Avraham. A commentary on the *Orach Chayim* of the *Shulchan Aruch* (see below), written by Rabbi Avraham Abeli ben Chayim Halevi Gombiner of Kalish (d. 1683), one of the great sages of Poland.

The Midrash. A generic term that usually refers to the non-legalistic teachings of the Rabbis of the Talmudic era. In the centuries following the final redaction of the Talmud (550 C.E.), much of this material was gathered into collections known as midrashim.

Midrash Rabbah (*Bereshis Rabbah, Shemos Rabbah, Devarim Rabbah,* cited). A midrashic work (see *The Midrash,* above) arranged by the amora, Rabbi Oshia Rabbah.

Midrash Tanchuma. A midrashic work (see *The Midrash,* above) written by the amora, Rabbi Tanchuma, in Israel.

Mishneh Torah. The most comprehensive and succinct guide to all the laws of the Torah and the greatest work of Rabbi Moshe ben Maimon (the Rambam, 1135-1204), also known as the *Yad ha-Chazakah.* Born in Cordova, Spain, to a distinguished Rabbinic family, the Rambam was the greatest codifier in Jewish history, as well as being a Rabbinic adjudicator, a Torah commentator, a philosopher, and a physician. The Rambam also wrote a commentary to the Mishnah, *Sefer ha-Mitzvos* (a classification of the 613 commandments), and *Moreh Nevuchim* (*Guide to the Perplexed,* intended to help the student who was struggling with the seeming contradictions between science and philosophy and the Torah).

Mor v'Shemesh. A chasidic classic by Rabbi Aharon ben Kalonimos of Krakow (d. 1882).

Perek Shirah. An early baraisa that shows how the entire creation sings praise to God, included in the midrashic work *Yalkut Shemoni* (see *The Midrash,* above).

Peri Tzaddik. A major chasidic work by Rabbi Tzaddok Hakohen of Lublin (d. 1905), who, while closely following the thinking of the Talmudic Sages and referring to history, created a unique form of Chasidism in his five volumes of sermons on the Shabbos and holiday portions.

Pirkei Avos (*Ethics of the Fathers*). A Mishnah tractate in the order of *Nezikin.* The Fathers are the early Talmudic Sages (c. 300 B.C.E.-200 C.E.) who composed the wise, moral sayings.

Pirkei d'Rabbi Eliezer. An important midrashic work (see *The Midrash,* above) by the school of Rabbi Eliezer ben Hyrcanus (c. 100 C.E.), first published in Constantinople in 1514.

Rashi. (Rabbi Shelomo ben Yitzchak Yarchi, 1040-1105). Author of the foremost commentaries on the *Chumash* and *Gemara.* His commentary on the *Chumash* is the first known Hebrew book published (in Rome, 1470). Rashi headed famous yeshiva academies in Troyes and Worms in France.

Reshis Chachmah. An ethics book written by Rabbi Eliyahu ben Moshe Vidash, a student of Rabbi Moshe Cordovero (see below, *Siddur Tefillah l'Moshe*).

Ruach Chayim. A commentary on *Pirkei Avos* (see above) by Rabbi Chayim of Volozhin (1749-1827), the leading student of the Vilna Gaon and the founder of the first great Lithuanian yeshiva, in Volozhin.

Sources

Seder Tu b'Shevat (*Peri Etz Hadar*). A course of study traditionally recited by Sephardic Jews during the eating of the Tu b'Shevat fruits.

Sha'ar ha-Kavanos. A kabbalistic work by Rabbi Chayim Vital (1547-1629).

Shir ha-Shirim. The Song of Songs, A love song to God by King Solomon.

Shulchan Aruch. The *Code of Jewish Law*, compiled by Rabbi Yosef Karo (1488-1575), a concentration of the halachic conclusions of the author's *Beis Yosef*, which is based on the *Tur* or *Arba'ah Turim* of Rabbi Ya'akov ben Asher. Rabbi Karo, who was born in Spain, became Chief Rabbi of Tzefas. He based his decisions on the Rambam, the Rosh, and the Rif. The *Shulchan Aruch* is composed of four parts:

ORACH CHAYIM contains all the laws that a Jew must perform daily (including on Shabbos and festivals), from the moment he opens his eyes in the morning until he closes them at night.

YOREH DE'AH contains all the laws regulating daily life that are not necessarily performed every day, such as kosher slaughter and the intricacies of kosher eating and drinking.

EVEN HA-EZER contains all the laws regulating relations between men and women.

CHOSHEN MISHPAT contains all the laws governing conduct between man and his fellow.

With the addition of the *Haga'ah*, glosses written by Rabbi Moshe Isserlis, who presents the Ashkenazic interpretation and tradition, the *Shulchan Aruch* became the standard halachic guide for all Jews until today.

Shulchan ha-Tahor. A large chasidic treatise on the moral correction made by eating with proper intention and blessings, written by Rabbi Aharon Roth, the founder of the Toldos Aharon dynasty.

Shulchan shel Arba'ah. A concise guide to the laws of eating and drinking at the weekday and Shabbos table, written by Rabbenu Bachya ben Asher (1263-1340), Rabbinical judge and preacher in Spain who wrote commentaries on the Torah and a kabbalistic work called *Kad ha-Kemach*.

Siddur Tefillah l'Moshe. The edition of the prayer book prepared by Rabbi Moshe Cordovero, the leading sixteenth-century kabbalist in Tzefas before Rabbi Yitzchak Luria.

The Talmud. The body of teaching that comprises the commentary and discussion of the early Talmudic Sages on the Mishnah of Rabbi Yehudah Hanasi. The study of the Mishnah was actively pursued in two centers: the Land of Israel and Babylon. As a result, two distinct versions of the Talmud emerged: the Jerusalem Talmud (whose compilation was completed in Tiveriya [Tiberias] at the beginning of the fifth century C.E.) and the Babylonian Talmud (whose compilation was completed at the end of the fifth century C.E.). Tractates of the Talmud cited in this book include: *Beitzah* — laws of festivals; *Berachos* — laws of blessings; *Kesubbos* — laws of marriage contracts; *Kilayim* — laws of forbidden hybridization and grafting; *Orlah* — laws on the first three years of fruit trees; *Pesachim* — laws of Pesach and the paschal sacrifice; *Rosh Hashanah* — laws of the New Year; *Shabbos* — laws of Shabbos; *Shevi'is* — agricultural laws for the sabbatical year; *Sotah* — laws of infidelity; *Ta'anis* — laws of fasting.

Tanna d'Vei Eliyahu. An early midrash (see *The Midrash*, above) attributed to the teachings of the prophet Eliyahu. First printed in Venice in 1598, its major and minor parts are called, in Aramaic, *Rabba* and *Zuta*.

Tehillim. A poetic work compiled by King David, including psalms of the ten elders: Adam, Malki Tzedek, Avraham, Moshe, Haimon, Yedusun, Asaf, and the three sons of Korach.

Tikkun Yissachar. A halachic work written by Rabbi Yissachar Sussan, one of the great sephardic rabbis of Tzefas during the time of Rabbi Yosef Karo and Rabbi Yitzchak Luria.

Yesod v'Shoresh ha-Avodah. A kabbalistic last will and testament prepared by Rabbi Alexander Ziskind for his students and published in Warsaw in 1913. In reviewing the moral conduct of his life, Rabbi Ziskind finds himself guilty of having eaten more than was necessary to sustain his study of Torah.

Zikkukin d'Nura u'Vi'urin d'Esha. A kabbalistic work, both exoteric and esoteric, by Rabbi Shemuel Hida, first published in Prague in 1675 and endorsed by the leading scholars of the time.

Ziv ha-Zohar. A commentary on the *Zohar* by Rabbi Yehudah Rosenberg from Warsaw, Poland.

Zohar. Meaning "splendor," the *Zohar* is the major work of kabbalah in the form of discussions of second-century Land of Israel rabbinical scholars, led by Rabbi Shimon bar Yochai.